SPECIFICATION WRITING

for Architects and Surveyors

Tenth edition

Christopher J. Willis
FRICS, FCIArb
and
J. Andrew Willis
BSc, ARICS

OXFORD

BSP PROFESSIONAL BOOKS

LONDON EDINBURGH BOSTON

MELBOURNE PARIS BERLIN VIENNA

Copyright © Arthur J. Willis and
    Christopher J. Willis 1953, 1958, 1962,
    1966, 1968, 1971, 1979, 1983
Copyright © Christopher J. Willis and
    J. Andrew Willis 1989, 1991

BSP Professional Books
A division of Blackwell Scientific
    Publications Ltd
Editorial offices:
Osney Mead, Oxford OX2 0EL
25 John Street, London WC1N 2BL
23 Ainslie Place, Edinburgh EH3 6AJ
3 Cambridge Center, Cambridge,
    MA 02142, USA
54 University Street, Carlton,
    Victoria 3053, Australia

First edition published in Great Britain by
    Crosby Lockwood & Son Ltd 1953
Reprinted 1954
Second edition published 1958
Third edition published 1962
Fourth edition published 1966
Fifth edition (metric) published 1968
Sixth edition published 1971
Reprinted by Crosby Lockwood Staples 1973,
    1975
Seventh edition published 1979
Seventh edition (revised) published by Granada
    Publishing 1981
Eighth edition published 1983
Ninth edition published by BSP Professional
    Books 1989
Tenth edition published 1991

Set by DP Photosetting, Aylesbury, Bucks
Printed and bound in Great Britain by
Hartnolls Ltd, Bodmin, Cornwall

DISTRIBUTORS
Marston Book Services Ltd
PO Box 87
Oxford OX2 0DT
(*Orders:* Tel: 0865 791155
        Fax: 0865 791927
        Telex: 837515)

USA
    Blackwell Scientific Publications, Inc.
    3 Cambridge Center
    Cambridge, MA 02142
    (*Orders:* Tel: (800) 759-6102)

Canada
    Oxford University Press
    70 Wynford Drive
    Don Mills
    Ontario M3C 1J9
    (*Orders:* Tel: (416) 441-2941)

Australia
    Blackwell Scientific Publications
    (Australia) Pty Ltd
    54 University Street
    Carlton, Victoria 3053
    (*Orders:* Tel: (03)347-0300)

British Library
Cataloguing in Publication Data
Willis, Christopher J. (Christopher James)
1928–
    Specification writing for architects and
    surveyors – 10th ed.
    1. Buildings. Construction. Specifications
    I. Title   II. Willis, J. Andrew
    692.3

ISBN 0–632–03202–2

Contents

Acknowledgements   iv
Preface to the tenth edition   v
Abbreviations used   vi
1 Purpose and use of the specification   1
2 Subject-matter   7
3 Form of the specification   14
4 The National Building Specification   23
5 Specification work sections   33

A   PRELIMINARIES/GENERAL CONDITIONS   35
B   COMPLETE BUILDINGS   39
C   DEMOLITION/ALTERATION/RENOVATION   40
D   GROUNDWORK   42
E   IN SITU CONCRETE/LARGE PRECAST CONCRETE   44
F   MASONRY   49
G   STRUCTURAL/CARCASSING METAL/TIMBER   54
H   CLADDING/COVERING   57
J   WATERPROOFING   62
K   LININGS/SHEATHING/DRY PARTITIONING   64
L   WINDOWS/DOORS/STAIRS   66
M   SURFACE FINISHES   71
N   FURNITURE/EQUIPMENT   78
P   BUILDING FABRIC SUNDRIES   81
Q   PAVING/PLANTING/FENCING/SITE FURNITURE   83
R   DISPOSAL SYSTEMS   86
S   PIPED SUPPLY SYSTEMS   91
T   MECHANICAL HEATING/COOLING/REFRIGERATION
    SYSTEMS   95
U   VENTILATION/AIR CONDITIONING SYSTEMS   97
V   ELECTRICAL SUPPLY/POWER/LIGHTING SYSTEMS   98
W   COMMUNICATIONS/SECURITY/CONTROL SYSTEMS   99
X   TRANSPORT SYSTEMS   100
Y   SERVICES REFERENCE SPECIFICATION   101
Z   BUILDING FABRIC REFERENCE SPECIFICATION   103

Appendix   Example specification   104
Index   135
Drawing   *inside back cover*

Acknowledgements

We are most grateful to Mr David Juniper DipArch, RIBA for permission to use his drawing and for his help in preparing the copy for reproduction and to Mr Tony Allott BArch, FRIBA for his assistance with the chapter on the NBS and the example specification and to National Building Specification Ltd for permission to reproduce samples of the NBS text and to use the Minor Works version as the basis for the Example Specification.

Specify To speak of or name something definitely or explicitly, to set down or state categorically or particularly
Shorter Oxford English Dictionary

'There's no place like home
If it's all to specification'
Comic song Arthur Askey, 1938

Preface to the tenth edition

One of the primary aims of this book when it was first published in 1953 was to encourage good specification writing by architects and surveyors. At that time it was common practice for specifications to be hand-written, albeit often using previous documentation suitably amended. Over the intervening years the practice of writing specifications fell into decline; on many occasions specifications became a matter of a few sheets of hastily drafted notes or more often it was a case of 'It's all on the drawings'.

Today, due to the advances in computer techniques, slowly at first but with gathering momentum, standard specifications have become the order of the day. Now architects and surveyors enjoy the benefits of having the facility to call up mark up copies of a standard specification to be adapted for each specific project.

Successive editions of this book have endeavoured to reflect this change. The seventh edition published in 1979 introduced a chapter on the National Building Specification and sundry references in the text have from time to time been made. The original aim of encouraging good specification however remains as it always was. This edition goes even further. The specification today is perhaps better described as drafted rather than written reflecting the change from pen, ink and typewriter to the amended mark up specification with a computer generated print out. This change is reflected in that, whilst retaining the term specification writer, we refer to his or her efforts as drafting.

A further instance of this change is in the Example Specification. This has now been redrafted using as a base the Minor Works Version of the National Building Specification. The steps necessary to be taken to amend a mark up draft are explained in Chapter 4.

The emphasis has therefore changed from the careful hand-drafted specification to the adaptation of a standard specification; however there remains the same need to ensure that nothing is missed.

In preparing this edition Europe has not been forgotten. The European Committee for Standardization will, no doubt, in due course draft European Standards and British Standards as we know them may well change. For the forseeable future however the use of British Standards will continue to be applicable.

The introduction of co-ordinated project information, the pressing demands of the industry and its clients for better documentation and the ensuing financial benefits together with the requirements of quality assurance and professional indemnity mean that specifications can be said to be more important than ever. The challenge of this edition is to reflect these changes and to emphasise that importance. We hope that our readers feel we have met this challenge.

                                                                    CJW
October 1990   JAW

Abbreviations used

BCIS   Building Cost Information Service
BEC   Building Employers' Confederation
BS   British Standard (of the BSI)
BSI   British Standards Institution
CAWS   Common Arrangement of Work Sections for
       building works
CCPI   Co-ordinating Committee for Project
       Information
CI/SfB Construction Indexing Samarbetskommitén
       for Byggnadsfrägor
CP   Code of Practice (published by BSI)
CPI   Co-ordinated Project Information
JCT   Joint Contracts Tribunal
NBS   National Building Specification
NES   National Engineering Specification
PSA   Property Services Agency
RIBA   Royal Institute of British Architects
RICS   Royal Institution of Chartered Surveyors
SMM   Standard Method of Measurement

1 Purpose and use of the specification

INTRODUCTION

A specification writer should not require model clauses to know, for instance, what size of fascia to use, how to specify kitchen cabinets or what weight or width of flashings should be used. These are matters which must be decided from a knowledge of building construction, the fundamental aspect, the aesthetic effect required and the cost. Specifications must not be drafted in a haphazard fashion just as the items are thought of, but must follow a system whereby those using a specification can visualise the whole building in advance, whether to measure its constituent parts for an estimate or find definite instructions for erecting the building.

A large proportion of the items in every specification concern matters common to all, varying only in detail to suit the ideas and designs of the individual architect: these items form the backbone of the lists given in Chapter 5 for each section. It is not possible to anticipate every item in every specification. Each building will have its own peculiarities which are fairly certain to present themselves clearly to the specification writer. If, however, a specification properly covers all the points mentioned which are relevant, it will stand high in intrinsic merit and, what is more important, practical value.

The scope of this book is limited to simple building work. Engineering works are so varied in their nature that their special requirements must be considered on their merits. One can, perhaps, speak of an average or simple building, but it is difficult to apply such terms to engineering work and in consequence only passing reference is made. Road work in this book is limited to probable requirements for site roads, courtyards etc., and drainage, excluding the special needs of sewers.

The best test for a specification is for the person who drafted it to go on an extended holiday whilst quantities are being prepared or, if there are to be no quantities, whilst the building is erected, leaving to an assistant routine replies for the quantity surveyor or the inspection of the works. How many architects would feel confident in so doing?

A building begins as a concept in the mind of the architect. The conception must be elaborated in the drawing office, adapted to practical considerations and then conveyed to a number of people who will co-operate in the erection of the building. Until the time comes when telepathy is a certain science, intentions can only be conveyed by specific instructions. Whether the instructions are conveyed to the contractor direct or through the quantity surveyor is immaterial: unless they are specific and complete without gaps and overlapping, there will be delays and mistakes, to the detriment of the client's interests. The person who drafts a specification is assumed to know what is wanted. Once it is known what is wanted all that is required is for it to be expressed fully, clearly and systematically.

WHAT IS A SPECIFICATION FOR?

Unless the writer grasps the purpose of the document, it cannot be prepared successfully. The specification may have three purposes, in each case in conjunction with the drawings:

- To be read by the contractor's estimator as the only information available on which to prepare a competitive tender.
- To be read by the quantity surveyor to enable a bill of quantities to be prepared as a basis for such competitive tenders.
- To be read by the clerk of works and the contractor's agent during the progress of the contract as the architect's instructions for carrying out the work.

THE SPECIFICATION AS A BASIS FOR TENDERS

In smaller contracts, usually those under about £100,000 in value, contractors prepare their tenders from drawings and specifications only. Estimators take their own measurements of the work from the drawings and build up their estimates relying on the specification for a full description of quality, materials and workmanship. Besides this, drawings and specifications, when read together, must indicate everything required to be included in the estimate. If anything is omitted, something that is required is not mentioned or shown, or very obviously necessary or implied, such work will not be part of the contract. If its carrying out is insisted upon, the contractor will be entitled to extra payment.

The writer of a specification for this purpose will, therefore, realise the importance of the work necessary. Instructions must be specific and crystal-clear and complete in detail. The specification will be one of the contract documents and is not to be hurriedly thrown together. It must have all the preciseness of an agreement (it will, in fact, be part of one) conveying exactly to the contractor what is wanted and protecting the building owner from claims for extra payment which would arise from vagueness and uncertainty.

THE SPECIFICATION FOR THE QUANTITY SURVEYOR

For contracts of a value of over about £100,000 it is usual for a bill of quantities to be supplied on behalf of the client if competitive tenders are being invited. The measuring work, which in the previous case would be done by all the tenderers, is in these circumstances done for them by the quantity surveyor who puts before them the facts, but each tenderer is left with the estimating, this being largely a matter of individual judgment.

In order that the quantity surveyor may prepare the bill, instructions must be given by the architect as complete as those required by the contractors when taking their own measurements and these instructions are conveyed in a specification. In this case the architect's specification is not usually a contract document, it can be less formal and convey the information in the form of notes. For certain standard clauses reference may be made to another contract. Whilst such a specification should be as complete as possible, omissions are not as vital as in the first case. The quantity surveyor will find the gaps, as in preparing the quantities every stage in the erection of the building has to be visualised and questions will arise whenever further information is required to complete the specification preambles which should be in CAWS order to enable easy reading with the measured items. It should be noted that where the architect's specification is not a contract document (as in the JCT 'with quantities' forms) the preambles must convey the specification information to enable the bills to 'fully describe and accurately represent the quantity and quality of the work' as required by the SMM.

THE SPECIFICATION FOR SITE AGENT AND CLERK OF WORKS

When the erection of a building starts the work will be supervised on behalf of the contractor by the site agent. On large projects a clerk of works will be employed to inspect on behalf of the employer, since constant inspection will be necessary and the architect is not expected to be continuously on the site. Both site agent and clerk of works require instructions and they take these, subject to any variations ordered by the architect, from the contract documents, i.e. drawings and specification or drawings and bill of quantities. Where quantities have been prepared, the quantity surveyor will have incorporated the specification in the descriptions or in the preambles in the bill. There is however, certain information required by the site agent and clerk of works, which will have been excluded from the bill. The location of the items, for instance, will not usually be mentioned in the bill because they do not normally affect price; however the site agent must have this information when it comes to erecting the building. There are also matters which must be conveyed as instructions to the site agent. For instance it may be required that floor joists shall not be spaced more than 300 mm apart. This the quantity surveyor will have duly noted in taking the measurements, but, having taken them accordingly, there is no reason to state the requirement in the bill. When it comes to erection, however, the site agent must have this direction which in this case would probably have been shown on the drawings.

THE CONTENTS

The specification is drafted to convey to the reader all the information about a proposed building which the architect cannot easily show on the drawings. For instance, the quality of a material to be used and the way pipes are to be joined together cannot be shown on a drawing, except by adding such full written notes or large-scale details that their main purpose is obscured. On the other hand without this supplementary information the estimator, working without quantities, cannot prepare the tender. If quantities are being supplied, the quantity surveyor is in equal difficulty in preparing them as the architect's wishes are not known.

ESSENTIALS IN WRITING

There are two essentials in drafting a specification:

(a) To know what one requires
(b) To be able to express it clearly

Many specifications fail for lack of (a). Such lack of knowledge has two causes:

(1) Insufficient thought
(2) Insufficient knowledge of building construction

If the architect has not thought about what is wanted, the estimator or quantity surveyor can hardly be expected to know. It must be remembered that every step in the carrying out of the work has to be visualised in advance by the estimator (or the quantity surveyor). If some requirement of the architect is not made clear it may quite possibly be missed and consequently result in a claim by the contractor for extra payment. The estimator in competitive tendering has not the time to work out what the architect or quantity surveyor has left undone, nor can the estimate be weighted to cover the item when the competitor's estimate may not. The quantity surveyor may realise the possibility of a claim arising and measure something to cover, but, may quite likely, guess wrongly. This will involve unnecessary adjustment of variations and extra expense to the employer.

Even if full thought has been given to the job it will still be unsatisfactory if the architect is lacking in knowledge of building construction. The students can only acquire this knowledge by hard work, constant visits to buildings under construction and by keeping up to date with information on new materials. The specification writer put in the place of the reader should be able, from the information available, to direct the operatives constructing the building. There should be no occasion to stop and say 'How am I to get over this difficulty?' or 'What do I put on top of this?'

The architect must have a knowledge of materials. If some branded article, e.g. fibreboard, plaster, plastic sheets, paint etc., is to be used, the architect must be thoroughly acquainted with the maker's recommendations, because what may apply to one brand may, quite possibly, not apply to others. Whilst one must remember that the anxiety of manufacturers to sell their products may make them optimistic, unless their recommendations are followed architects may find themselves blamed when defects appear.

In short, the drafting of a specification by the architect is nothing more than setting down what is required when it has been fully thought out. If it is known, say, that a timber fascia 175 mm wide would cover the ends of the timbers and be satisfactory aesthetically, that if 16 mm thick it will probably curl or split, if 40 mm thick money is being wasted, that it can be securely fixed to the particular roof construction by driving nails through it, that the nails must be driven into the holding material for a depth at least equal to the thickness of the fascia, that nails should be punched in and stopped or they will rust through the paint – then, if put in plain English, it is possible to explain precisely what is required.

Granted that the writer can specify the fascia referred to above the next important thing is completeness. Have all the varieties of fascias and all the members of the roof construction been specified? all carpentry items? and so on? Chapter 5 sets out the main sub-divisions of each work section with the essential points to be mentioned for each. The writer in following through the lists must consider which items apply to the particular case and then say what is wanted about each.

FOUNDATIONS

A possible uncertainty, which needs special consideration in specifications for tender where no quantities are supplied, is depth of foundations. The drawings and specifications read together will determine the extent of the contract work. They should either be definite, when any variation would be adjustable, or it should be stated that the whole will be measured and valued as done up to a specified level. The attention of the tenderer may be specifically drawn to the need for a schedule of rates to be prepared with a view to such measurement. The schedule will naturally follow the tenderer's method of estimating, so it is difficult to lay down particular requirements as to its form.

2 Subject-matter

Some of the information required of the architect is best shown on the drawings, and being so shown, is not required in the specification. The CPI Code for Production Drawings sets out the links that can be achieved by common arrangement between specification and drawings. The architect should see that the following are all shown on the drawings:

- Ground levels of the site
- Floor levels related to ground levels
- Figured dimensions:
    - (a) walls over all on plans
    - (b) inside dimensions of rooms
    - (c) heights
    - (d) (in the case of steel-framed buildings) centre to centre of stanchions and relation of steelwork lines to wall and floor surfaces
    - (e) setting out of openings
- Position of steps in concrete foundations
- Room titles (or serial numbers)
- Opening portions of windows
- Direction of opening of doors
- Runs of service pipes
- Position of cupboards or other fittings
- Position of electric points

It will also simplify reference in the specification if windows and doors are given serial numbers in one or separate series. The numbering should start in one corner of the plan (usually top left) and continue clockwise.

It is not usually necessary to incorporate sketches in a specification, as anything that needs illustration in that way would be shown on the drawings and reference to the drawing number would be sufficient.

SUBDIVISION

The traditional subdivision in the case of a new building was into recognised 'Trade Sections'. Now with the introduction of Common Arrangement they will be structured in CAWS order. Work should be specified in its proper section, but where several sections are involved cross-references to clause numbers should be given.

In the case of alteration work, whilst Common Arrangement has sections for Demolition (C10) and Works on Site and Spot items (C20) it is sometimes more useful to subdivide the specification according to rooms or parts of the building, so that everything in connection with that room or part is together. Or a combination of the two systems may be adopted to save unnecessary repetition, namely, to specify the alteration work room by room but keep in a separate section all new work in connection classified into work sections (the description of which might otherwise have to be repeated many times). Each alteration job must be considered on its merits and that system adopted which seems to suit that particular scheme best.

WORKS OF ALTERATION

In specifying works of alteration by rooms or by parts of a building one should take each room in a sequence which can conveniently be followed walking round the building, thus putting oneself in the position of the contractor's estimator and consider what information is necessary for quoting a price. The impossible should not be attempted and if it is not reasonable for the estimator to anticipate the work required a provisional sum should be given which will in due course be adjusted against actual cost.

A point often not visualised sufficiently by specification writers is the amount of damage that will be caused by traffic, dumping of materials, vibration etc. One of the commonest arguments over alteration jobs is how much plaster should have been renewed under the contract. Inherent defects, such as a bad key, are apt to reveal themselves unexpectedly during the progress of the work and the contractor will disclaim liability for them.

PC PRICES AND PROVISIONAL SUMS

There is nearly always certain work required on a building which is outside the sphere of the normal contractor and necessitates the introduction of a specialist on the site. Such work may vary from plastering or plumbing which some contractors do undertake with their own staff, to electrical work which is only occasionally part of a contractor's business. Such work is let by the contractor as a sub-contract. In the former more ordinary trades it is usually left to the contractor to make his own arrangements, but in such matters as electrical work, central heating, lifts etc., the selection of the firm will probably be made by the architect. Under the terms of the standard forms of contract firms carrying out this latter work become 'nominated sub-contractors' ('named sub-contractors' in the case of the JCT Intermediate Form of Contract) and, though the contractor remains responsible for their work, the architect controls the appointment. In the specification the tenderers are told to provide a PC sum of £x for the work, and the sum so included in the tender will be subject to adjustment against the specialist's account.

Such nominated, or named, sub-contractors are essentially firms doing work on the site. It often happens, however, that the architect wants to select certain materials or goods which the contractor is to fix. What is wanted may be known but it may be necessary to defer decision as to the exact model or make until the contract is let. If so, again, tenderers will be given a figure to include subject to adjustment as their services are restricted to supply only: such firms are known as 'nominated suppliers'.

Sums so included in a tender subject to adjustment are termed 'provisional sums' or 'prime cost sums'. Provisional sums are lump sums given provisionally i.e. subject to adjustment, to include all profit, attendance etc., which, when the adjustment is made, will be allowed in accordance with the terms of the contract governing variations. Prime cost sums (usually abbreviated to PC sums) are sums deemed for the purpose of the tender to be the prime cost (basic cost before addition of overhead charges and profit) to the contractor: if the actual cost is more or less, adjustment will be made accordingly, both of the expenditure and of any profit, attendance on sub-contractors etc., added in the tender.

The architect is responsible for obtaining the quotations from nominated sub-contractors and suppliers.

BUILDING REGULATIONS

Responsibility that the work shown and specified complies with the regulations of controlling authorities is for the architect. Existing local bye-laws were replaced as from 1 February 1966 by Building Regulations (Building Regulations – HMSO) which were to apply to the whole of England and Wales, except the Inner London Boroughs where building was still to be controlled by the London Building Acts. With the dissolution of the Greater London Council the London Building Act was repealed and the Building Regulations now apply equally in London.

Apart from this, water authorities have regulations specifying, for instance, minimum strengths of pipes. To say 'that the pipes are to be of the strengths required by the Water Authority' is not good enough. Requirements as to strength often differ with the pressure at the particular point in the supply system: the architect should ascertain this information and not expect tenderers to make these investigations.

PROVISIONAL SUMS FOR STATUTORY CHARGES

In the same way as for specialists' work provisional sums have to be included in a specification for work which local authorities, nationalised and privatised boards etc. have to carry out under statutory or similar powers, for example the connections of drains to public sewers, the bringing in to the premises of water, gas or electric services. The extent of work done by such authorities varies. A gas board will probably bring their main up to a meter within the building, whereas a water authority may only bring their supply up to the boundary of the property. A local authority may allow a contractor to break up a road or they may insist on doing this themselves. The specification must be quite clear as to how much work is covered by the provisional sum and how much the contractor has to do. Enquiry should be made of the authority concerned and an estimate obtained, any doubt as to the extent of the work being clarified with them. Payment for charges of these authorities is due to the contractor and these provisional sums do not include for cash discount, as do those for nominated sub-contractors. If however the same authorities undertake further work such as the electric wiring of the building they will do so as nominated sub-contractors on the same basis as private firms.

USE OF STANDARD SPECIFICATIONS AND CODES OF PRACTICE

The extent to which standard documents should be referred to in a specification is sometimes difficult to decide. The British Standards Institution (BSI) publishes standards for a very wide range of materials. Many of them are prepared with a view to use for local authority housing contracts, the standard for which may not be high enough for some other types of building. Codes of practice relating to workmanship in various trades are also published by the BSI. A thorough knowledge of these standards and codes would need almost a life's work and is not a practical possibility for the ordinary professional: moreover, few contractors will have a complete range of them in their office. On the other hand, merchants supplying, say, clayware drainage goods or specialists such as asphalt laying firms would be familiar with the standards and codes applicable to their particular line.

Generally speaking it is advisable to refer to British Standards for the more usual materials and Codes of Practice can be incorporated where considered useful, but it is most important in either case to be conversant with the terms of the document quoted. It is not sufficient to say 'All materials are to be in accordance with the relevant British Standard' nor 'that all work is to comply with the Codes of Practice issued by the BSI', without stating the reference number of the particular standard or code. Even where reference numbers are quoted a BS may have subdivisions for different designs or qualities of the same article. Provided that in such cases reference is made to the appropriate subdivision, a BS number may help considerably in shortening descriptions. Similarly an examination of one of the Codes of Practice may reveal alternatives or some requirement with which there may be reason to disagree. Many of the Codes of Practice have now been converted to standards and it is the policy of the BSI to continue this process. The use of references to these documents must not be allowed to encourage laziness.

WORKMANSHIP

The importance of good workmanship on building sites is self-evident and the need to specify this important aspect adequately cannot be over-emphasised, but adequate specification has in the past never proved easy to achieve. Realising this difficulty, BSI have brought out BS 8000: Workmanship on Building Sites. This BS is a code of practice which brings together tried and tested procedures for a variety of building operations.

BS 8000 is in fifteen parts and each part covers a particular topic, setting out both general and specific recommendations on the way things should be done. Prepared as it is in CAWS order, cross referencing is simple. Examples of the use of BS 8000 in an actual specification will be found in the example specification (pages 105–133).

BS 8000 consists of the following parts:

Part   Code of Practice for
1   Excavation and filling
2   Concrete work:
        2.1 mixing and transporting concrete
        2.2 placing, compaction and curing
3   Masonry
4   Waterproofing
5   Carpentry, joinery and general fixings
6   Slating and tiling of roofs and cladding
7   Glazing
8   Plasterboard partitions and dry linings
9   Cement/sand floor screeds and concrete floor toppings
10   Plastering and rendering
11   Wall and floor tiling:
        11.1 ceramic tiles, terrazzo tiles and mosaics
        11.2 natural stone tiles
12   Decorative wall coverings and painting
13   Above ground drainage and sanitary appliances
14   Below ground drainage
15   Hot and cold water services (domestic scale).

In the schedules of specification work sections (Chapter 5) the allocation of BS 8000 between the relevant CAWS is shown in each case at the end of the summary of the CAWS.

BUILDING OWNER'S OWN MATERIALS

It sometimes happens that the contract is to include for the fixing of materials supplied by the building owner. This may be on a large scale when public authorities take advantage of the cheaper rates obtainable by bulk buying, or just because the building owner has picked up some old panelling or a fireplace which he wants incorporated in the building. In specifying such work it must be made clear that this material will be supplied to the contractor and delivered to the job without expense.

PRELIMINARY ITEMS

The preliminary items will cover all matters of a general nature or applying to the sections generally. They include any definitions and refer to such matters as conditions of contract, working rules, general organisation of the job, provision of plant, sheds, water, temporary lighting, temporary roads, insurances etc. The detailed Common Arrangement list will be found in Chapter 5. The conditions of contract being incorporated in the specification by reference, need not be repeated in full, but it may be necessary to amplify them by specific provisions, such as accommodation for the clerk of works, administrative directions as to preparation of daywork sheets or price adjustment statements etc.

KEEPING UP TO DATE

It is most important for those drafting specifications to keep up to date with developments. Not only must changes in such matters as the various forms of contract and the working rules of the industry be watched, but it is necessary to keep abreast with the use of new materials and study their methods of fixing, and not forgetting to take note when materials become obsolete. The development of modern materials has done away with many of the old traditional materials such as hand made stopping and white lead.

If an architect or surveyor is a subscriber to a standard specification service such as NBS then, as described in Chapter 4, they can follow these changes in the updated sheets received. If not, however, they will need to watch their professional journal, new publications of interest and changes in practice either obligatory or recommended. Subscription services such as BCIS are available which provide helpful information. It may mean some duplication but this does no harm: in fact repetition helps to impress.

It is physically impossible to master the flood of literature on technical matters which comes from the presses, but to watch the titles with only a vague idea of the subject-matter may at some later date prove valuable. It is much better to spend time noting what information is available than trying to master the detail of something which may never be wanted. Persons who know where to put their finger on information when it is wanted are of much more value (except unfortunately in examinations) than the ones who try to cram facts into their heads.

3 Form of the specification

AUTHORSHIP

The specification, if not drafted by the architect, should be drafted by an assistant who has worked on the drawings and knows the conditions and requirements of the job. Ideally, a specification should be prepared in parallel with the preparation of the drawings. Some offices operate a system whereby a 'specification writer' is employed solely to draft specifications. Such a person, to do the job properly, has to spend much time in studying the drawings to get a grasp of each scheme and probably take up the time of the architect or assistants in asking questions which have already been settled, but answers to which may not be obvious from the drawings. There is therefore something to be said for the person who has seen the thrashing out of the scheme through all its stages in preparation of the drawings writing the specification.

COMPOSITION AND STYLE

If the specification is being drafted by hand rather than using a standard specification it need not be a work of literature written in the flowing periods of Macaulay: it is essentially a document for quick reference and quick understanding. This being so, it should be divided into short paragraphs with clear headings and arranged in a systematic order. Nevertheless, the drafting must be grammatical and properly punctuated (for good punctuation does much to help clear understanding). If it is drafted in a hurry without time spared for reading through, it is bound to show defects and uncertainties which the writer could easily have avoided. It may be contended that bad style or spelling are not important if the words are understood, but they do show slovenliness which reflects on the writer.

The writer should use language that is plain and straightforward, bearing in mind that he is giving orders which must not be misunderstood. Every word should mean something, and the phrasing must be definite, except only where alternatives are intentionally left to the contractor.

The best rule for punctuation is to imagine reading the document aloud and putting the stops where natural pauses occur either for breath or for a change of tone (e.g. to indicate parenthesis or a conditional clause). Sentences should be short: separate sentences with a colon or semicolon between are clearer than a long sentence divided by commas into clauses the construction of which becomes involved.

Shortcomings in drafting, together with a lack of compatibility with other project information, have been highlighted (Project Information Group report – 1979) as one of the prime causes of disruption of building operations on site leading as they do so often to delays and subsequent loss and expense claims. In order to improve the situation the Co-ordinating Committee for Project Information (CCPI) was set up and after consultation with all interested parties produced a Common Arrangement of Work Sections for Building Works (CAWS) and a Code for Project Specification writing. They also produced a similar code for Production Drawings and worked in conjunction with the producers of SMM 7. The last two of these documents are mainly outside the scope of this book: the first two are of prime relevance.

COMMON ARRANGEMENT OF WORK SECTIONS

The purpose of CAWS, as set out in its introduction, is to define an efficient and generally acceptable identical arrangement for specifications and bills of quantities.

The main advantages are:

- Easier distribution of information, particularly in the dissemination of information to sub-contractors: one of the prime objectives in structuring the sections was that the requirements of sub-contractors should not only be recognised but kept together in relatively small tight packages
- More effective reading together of documents. Use of CAWS coding allows the specification to be directly linked to the bill of quantities descriptions: cutting down the descriptions in the latter whilst still giving all the information contained within the former
- Greater consistency achieved by implementation of the above advantages. The site agent and clerk of works can be confident that when they compare the drawings with the specification and both with the bill of quantities no longer will they have to ask the question 'Which is right?'

CAWS is a system based on the concept of work sections. To avoid boundary problems between similar or related work sections, CAWS gives, for each section, a list of what is included and what is excluded, stating the appropriate sections where the excluded items can be found.

CAWS has a hierarchical arrangement in three levels for instance:

- Level 1 R   Disposal systems
- Level 2 R1   Drainage
- Level 3 R10 Rainwater pipework/gutters

There are 24 Level 1 group headings, 150 work sections for building fabric and 120 work sections for services. Although very much depending on size and complexity, no single project will need more than a fraction of this number – perhaps as a very general average 25–30%. Only level 1 and level 3 are normally used in specifications and bills of quantities. Level 2 indicates the structure, and helps with the management of the notation. New work sections can be inserted quite simply without the need for extensive renumbering.

PROJECT SPECIFICATION CODE

The purpose of this code is to help the practitioner review and upgrade their specification practice. The code is divided into three parts:

- Part A   General principles of specification writing
- Part B   Guidance on coverage
- Part C   Libraries of specification clauses.

Each part sets out detailed guidance on how the main aims of the code can be achieved in practice. As with Chapter 5 of this book CAWS sections are looked at and lists of items for consideration are given. Chapter 5 however goes one stage further by listing the relevant British Standards.

The remainder of this chapter covers matters such as terminology, consistency, procedure in drafting, underlining, headings, numbering, indexing and standardisation.

TERMINOLOGY

The principles of terminology are described in BS 3669 but of more practical importance is BS 6100: Glossary of Building and Civil Engineering Terms, a detailed specification in six parts covering all sections of building and civil engineering construction. Terminology required for retrieval purposes is best found in a thesaurus. This is a document which indicates terms authorised for use in indexing. Terms that may not be used are cross-referenced to those which may be, and relationships between indexing terms are shown. Most thesauri are designed for use within a particular subject field or discipline, or are associated with a particular data base. The Construction Industry Thesaurus published by the Department of Environment, has been produced for use in the UK construction industry and contains some 9000 entries. There are two listings – an alphabetical list of terms and their synonyms and a classified display showing the more important relationships between terms. Ten categories are used:

(1) physical forms of presentation (for indicating whether a document is a report, a book, a piece of trade literature)
(2) peripheral subjects (i.e. those not unique to the construction industry, e.g. training, environment)
(3) time
(4) place (i.e. physical location)
(5) properties and measures
(6) agents of construction (i.e. people, plant)
(7) operations and processes
(8) materials
(9) parts of construction works
(10) construction works

PROCEDURE IN DRAFTING

It may be that the drafting of 'Preliminary Items' will be left to the end: they are almost independent of work in the sections and can be deferred. Within each section the materials and workmanship clauses are also best left until the actual work has been specified. Until this is done it is difficult to see exactly what materials and workmanship require description.

In thinking of the building by sections the ground works will be the first items to be put down and all the varieties must be thought of. Similarly with concrete, there will be foundations, beds, lintels and other items all to be considered.

Working according to sections of the building, the first matter will be the clearing of the site: then will follow foundations i.e. everything up to damp proof course level or equivalent including the concrete and masonry as well as the groundworks. Plenty of space will be allowed for coming back to these sections when dealing with the superstructure.

In the final form of the specification the clauses should generally be in the CAWS order given in Chapter 5 and any necessary transfers can be made on the draft by the use of symbols and cross references to make quite clear what alterations in order are to be made.

UNDERLINING

Caution is needed in the use of underlining. Tenderers are apt to skip the Preliminary Items and descriptions of materials and workmanship to save time, assuming that requirements are normal, a dangerous practice putting themselves very much at risk, but being done just the same. To underline important clauses almost makes matters worse, as, though attracted to the underlined words, the estimator tends to pay less attention to the rest. Underlining adds nothing legally to words which are already binding.

CLAUSE HEADINGS AND NUMBERING

Quick reference is very important in specifications. Clauses should, therefore, have headings to indicate their contents. A clause may well have more than one paragraph and unless there is a close relation between paragraphs it is better that they are each made a separate clause with its own number.

CONSISTENCY

It is important that the specification should be consistent in all its parts, though this may sometimes be difficult when the drafting is spread over any length of time. It is obvious that in interpretation of a document confusion is bound to arise if the same word or expression is used in different senses in different parts of the document, and conversely if different words or expressions are used with the same meaning.

Another example of inconsistency often met with is in the order in which dimensions are given. There is a generally accepted custom in the building trade that they shall be given in this order: length, width (or depth on bed), height. This is not universal, for it is pedantic or eccentric to talk of 3″ × 6″ steel joists when one has always heard them spoken of as 6″ × 3″, and, though one will hear of 50 × 100 mm wood rafter, they are more usually called 100 × 50 mm. Still there are occasions when a well understood order is important. A 450 × 150 mm lintel fair on both faces has 0.30 sq. m of fair face per lineal metre, whereas a 150 × 450 mm lintel (being 150 mm on bed and 450 mm high) would have 0.90 sq. m per lineal metre. The steel window manufacturers, however, always give the height followed by the width, and care is necessary when asking for quotations from such firms to state clearly which is width and which is height.

Lack of consistency also appears when timber is described sometimes as 'finished' and sometimes by basic sizes. If finished sizes are given a calculation will have to be made by the estimator each time to find the commercial sizes to which the buying is necessarily restricted. The most usual thicknesses for softwood are 25 mm, 30 mm, 40 mm, 50 mm and 75 mm. The recognised allowances from these nominal thicknesses for thickness as finished on the job are 3.20 mm for each sawn face. The quantity surveyor usually describes the items in the bill by basic sizes and confusion is likely to arise if the architect in specification and drawings given to the surveyor does not do the same.

The draft of a specification whether hand-written or produced from a word-processor will have to be prepared in a form suitable for final reproduction. To dictate it, except as a rough first draft to be put into shape later, is practically impossible. In preparing a draft plenty of space should be taken: it is easy enough to close up a draft, but to decipher an overcrowded one having alterations in wording and order can be extremely difficult. The specification has traditionally been arranged in trade order, now with the introduction of common arrangement, the order will be that adopted in CAWS.

Clauses should be numbered serially using the CAWS reference number with subservient sectional numbering. A liberal use should be made of cross referencing when it facilitates explanation. Given sectional numbering, e.g. A50.01, additional clauses can be inserted at the end of each section without disturbing the numbering throughout. The form in which it is suggested a specification should be written will be seen in the Appendix.

SCHEDULES

Schedules are an invaluable part of a specification for all but the smallest buildings, particularly in drawing distinctions between different treatments, e.g. to show which rooms have papered walls and which painted, where the different types of doors are and what ironmongery is to be fitted to each. They give, so to speak, a bird's-eye view of the requirements, fuller detail of which can be found by looking up the relevant paragraphs. They are especially useful as a supplement to bills of quantities when their items are referenced to the items in the bill. Instead of having to read long paragraphs of descriptions one can quickly trace the location of the items in the bill.

Schedules are sometimes prepared in the same way as drawings so that prints can be taken from them and included with the set of drawings. They are not then required in the specification but will be read with it, and, of course, the matter they contain need not be repeated.

INDEX

An index is a very useful adjunct to a specification. If nothing else is done a table of contents setting out the sections and sub-divisions thereof should precede page 1 so that quick reference can at any rate be made to the section of the specification required. A detailed index of all items means time and is hardly justified for a small specification; where each section has only two or three pages a quick glance down the headings will fairly certainly find the required item. In an extensive specification, however, a detailed index is undoubtedly useful and may be thought worthy of the trouble but in today's competitive climate it could be said to be an expensive luxury. A specimen table of contents is included in the example specification in the Appendix.

STANDARDISATION OF FORM

Standard specifications can take two forms. There are specifications like the National Building Specification (see Chapter 4) which are primarily a library of clauses which, as will be described, can be used to build up a working specification. Careful coding of the clauses permits the writer to refer simply to the relevant number or code and the typist or computer operator can do the rest. The second form of standard specification is one prepared with plenty of space for alterations and additions and a number of copies can be duplicated to serve as the draft for each project. This is done by government departments and local authorities where, for instance crown offices or schools were to be built in substantial numbers over several years, with similar methods of construction and general features. In using this form of standard specification great care must be taken. It is easy for something inapplicable to be left in, which, when duplicated into the individual specifications leaves no indication of being an oversight and looks silly. There may be alternatives in the standard draft one of which is to be deleted. The authors have before now come across such clauses as 'Facings to be in English/Flemish bond' or 'Plastering to be two/three coat work', showing lack of care and perhaps excessive haste in drafting. It is easy, too, when drafting from a standard specification like this to overlook items specially applicable to the particular project, which the standard specification never contemplated.

The disadvantage of a standard specification to be adapted for each project is that it tends to make the brain lazy. Instead of the writer's mind being alert on the job as it should be, a semi-mechanical process tends to be carried out based on other people's thinking.

LINK WITH BILLS OF QUANTITIES

As was mentioned in Chapter 1, the bill of quantities prepared by the quantity surveyor will have incorporated the specification matter, which, therefore, need not be repeated in a separate document. With the introduction of bills of quantities prepared in Common Arrangement order, cross-referencing to the specification is so straightforward that even more repetition is avoided. If the drawings, too, have CAWS references the ultimate aim of the information contained in the specification equalling that shown on the drawings equalling the bill descriptions will become much nearer to being achieved. The supplementary information as to location etc., required by the site agent and the clerk of works can be set out in a form of notes referenced to the items in the bill of quantities.

REPRODUCTION

Traditionally specifications were produced by type and carbon when only one or two contractors were tendering or by typing stencils and duplicating when larger numbers were involved. Today however the more usual form is for the information to be stored in a computerised retrieval system and called off for each project, drafted, adapted or amended as the case may be and then printed either 'one off', for subsequent photo-copying, or by a multiple printing process contained within the retrieval system.

Protective covers should be used as the specification will receive a good deal of handling, especially if there are no bills of quantities and it is the sole document to interpret the drawings. It is more convenient to handle if stapled or bound down the left-hand side so that it can be opened like a book. A pin through the top left-hand corner makes pages awkward to turn over and inclined to tear.

PROOFS

Reproduction by any means must be examined before making up or binding, so that corrections can be made; obvious mistakes, pages out of order or upside down etc., give a very poor impression. Reading a draft, particularly if it has been produced by hand, the non-technical typist or printer can easily make mistakes which will look foolish, e.g. 'core' for 'cove' or 'hoarding' for 'boarding'. Though readers may guess the error, there might be cases where they will be puzzled by the misprint.

4 The National Building Specification

The National Building Specification (NBS) is not a standard specification. It is a large library of specification clauses all of which are optional, many are direct alternatives, and which in many cases require the insertion of additional information. NBS thus facilitates the production of specification text specific to each project, including all relevant matters and excluding text which does not apply.

The existence of NBS underlines the ambiguity that the building industry gives to the word specification. To most architects it means the description of the quality of materials and workmanship required in the building. To most quantity surveyors it has come to mean the description of the work required (Schedule of Work) where quantities are not provided. NBS could be thought of by the quantity surveyor as National Building Preambles.

NBS is available only as a subscription service, and in this way it is kept up to date by issue of new material, several times a year, for insertion into the loose-leaf ring binders. Until 1988 NBS was available in either CI/Sfb or SMM6 order, but these have been discontinued. NBS is now available only in the Common Arrangement of Work Sections, matching SMM7 and complying fully with the recommendations of the CPI Code of Procedure for Project Specification referred to in Chapter 3. There are three versions of the text, the 'Standard Version', an abridged 'Intermediate Version' and a 'Minor Works Version' published in 1990.

The range of specification clauses offered is wide and care must be taken to include only those which are required for the particular project. It is important to specify only those requirements which one is prepared to enforce, for as in traditional specification writing the inclusion of clauses which will not, or cannot, be enforced undermines the authority of the document as a whole.

NBS includes against most of its clauses guidance notes which draw attention to other documents, alternative and related clauses, and indicate the type of additional information which is required to complete a clause. Expendable copies of NBS work sections are available for 'mark up' and these do not have the guidance notes. Also, the NBS clauses are available on disc to suit all types of word processor or computer in common use.

The recommended procedure for using NBS is as described in the CPI Project Specification Code. A list of the specification sections should be prepared and an expendable copy of those sections obtained. The responsibility for writing particular sections should be decided, essentially according to who has responsibility for detailed design.

For each section of the specification the NBS clauses and accompanying guidance notes should be read, together with the appropriate parts of the relevant Code of Practice and other reference documents. This can be time consuming, but it is essential if the finished specification is to be technically sound.

The expendable copy of the NBS clauses can then be marked up, building up the project specification clause by clause. This is best done concurrently with preparation of the drawings and may be an intermittent activity spread over several days or even weeks. At the end of the process it is important to check through to ensure that the specification has been completed. Each section should be reviewed in general terms to ensure that it is appropriate to the needs of the job – it should be abbreviated or elaborated as thought fit.

The specification should be prepared before bills of quantities are prepared, and in parallel with the production drawings so that, for example, the drawings for the main structure and the specification sections for concrete and brickwork are given to the quantity surveyor at the same time. It is usually advantageous to supply the specification to the quantity surveyor in draft form, because as the first user of the document he or she will therefore be likely to discover any omissions or discrepancies. These can then be corrected before the specification is issued to tenderers as part of the bills of quantities.

A specimen example of NBS Intermediate Version text is given on pages 25–32 showing how it is marked up for a particular project. The example completed specification on pages 105–133 has been drafted using the NBS Minor Works Version. It will be clear from these that the system encourages standardisation, but at the same time provides a framework for describing the particular requirements of each project. The completed specification is set out in a way which facilitates cross-reference from the drawings and bill descriptions, e.g. 'Facing brickwork F10/110.'

NBS is a very useful tool for use by the design team and produces comprehensive, concise and constructive specifications to support the information given on drawings and in measured items.

F10

BRICK/BLOCK WALLING

SCOPE

This section covers the laying of bricks and blocks of clay, concrete and calcium silicate in courses on a mortar bed to form walls, partitions, chimneys, plinths, boiler seatings, etc. Other sections related to brick/block walling are:

- F20 Natural stone rubble walling
- F21 Natural stone ashlar walling/dressings
- F30 Accessories/Sundry items for brick/block/stone walling
- F31 Precast concrete sills/lintels/copings/features
- Z21 Mortars.

Simple reconstructed stonework, of the type intended for laying by general bricklayers, is included in this section (see clause 290).

GENERAL GUIDANCE ON SPECIFYING TYPES OF WALLING

1 USING THE TYPES OF WALLING CLAUSES

A range of clauses is included at the beginning of this section which can be used to specify the various types of brick/block walling, namely:

CLAY FACING BRICKWORK
CALCIUM SILICATE FACING BRICKWORK
CONCRETE FACING BRICKWORK
SECOND HAND FACING BRICKWORK
CONCRETE FACING BLOCKWORK
RECONSTRUCTED STONEWORK
CLAY COMMON BRICKWORK
CALCIUM SILICATE COMMON BRICKWORK
CONCRETE COMMON BRICKWORK
CONCRETE COMMON BLOCKWORK
ENGINEERING BRICKWORK
DAMP PROOF COURSE BRICKWORK

Complete a clause for each variation of brickwork and blockwork, deleting items which do not apply, e.g.

110   CLAY FACING BRICKWORK *ABOVE DPC*:
- Bricks: To BS 3921.
  Manufacturer and reference: *Birtley Brick Co: Blue Multis.*
  ~~Special shapes:~~ . . . .
- Mortar: As section Z21.
  Mix: *1:1:6 cement:lime:sand.*
  ~~Special colour:~~ . . . .
- Bond: *Half lap stretcher.*
- Joints: *Bucket handle.*
- Features: *Soldier course over openings.*

Clauses can be repeated as necessary. If a clause is repeated it is quite likely that this is because of a change in brick or mortar or bond or joints, but unlikely that all of these elements will change. In other words, repetition of the same information is likely. This can be overcome by referring to a previous clause, e.g.

110A CLAY FACING BRICKWORK *BELOW DPC*:
- Bricks: To BS 3921.
  Manufacturer and reference: *As F10/110.*
  ~~Special shapes:~~ . . . .
- Mortar: As section Z21.
  Mix: *1:½:4 with sulphate resisting cement.*
  ~~Special colour:~~ . . . .
- Bond: *As F10/110.*
- Joints: *As F10/110.*
- Features: *As F10/110.*

The guidance notes below apply generally and are arranged in the same sequence as the clause subheadings.

2 CLAUSE HEADINGS

These should describe the use and/or location of the brick/blockwork in a way which will be helpful to the Contractor, e.g.
CLAY FACING BRICKWORK *ABOVE DPC ON HOUSE TYPES 5 AND 7*:
CONCRETE FACING BLOCKWORK *IN CORRIDORS*:
ENGINEERING BRICKWORK *FOR MANHOLES*:

The Contractor will normally be looking first for information on the drawings and then to the specification. Therefore the clause heading need not be absolutely precise but more a confirmation that the clause is the correct one for the situation identified and/or cross-referenced on the drawings.

3 CLAY BRICKS

The last revision of BS 3921 introduced major changes in the classification of clay bricks, which are now designated according to frost resistance and soluble salt content:

Designation	Frost resistance	Soluble salt content
FL	Resistant	Low
FN	Resistant	Normal
ML	Moderately resistant	Low
MN	Moderately resistant	Normal
OL	Not resistant	Low
ON	Not resistant	Normal

BS 3921 specifies a maximum limit for soluble salt content in bricks designated 'Low' but not for 'Normal'.

Apart from engineering and damp proof course bricks, BS 3921 no longer classifies bricks by compressive strength.

4 CALCIUM SILICATE BRICKS

These should comply with BS 187. Apart from strength Class 2 (which, anyway, is not generally available) calcium silicate bricks have good frost resistance, even when saturated. Classes 3 to 7 can be used in any situation with the exceptions of:
- Cappings, copings and sills: Minimum class 4
- Earth retaining walls not water-proofed on the retaining side: Minimum class 4
- Manholes with foul effluent in continuous contact with the brickwork: Minimum class 7
- Damp proof courses: Not suitable.

See BS 5628:Part 3, table 13.

5 CONCRETE BRICKS

These should comply with BS 6073:Part 1. This standard does not give recommendations as to suitability for particular purposes.

Concrete bricks should not be used in contact with ground from which there is danger of sulphate attack unless the units are protected or have been specifically made for this purpose, i.e. with sulphate resisting cement and/or a certain minimum cement content – see BRE Digest 250.

Durability is related to the strength of the bricks and requirements vary greatly, depending on the situation. For detailed guidance see BS 5628:Part 3, table 13.

6 CONCRETE BLOCKS

BS 6073:Part 1 does not specify functional properties such as thermal conductivity, nor does it give recommendations as to suitability for particular purposes – for guidance on selection of blocks see:
- 'Products in practice supplement: Bricks and blocks', The Architects' Journal December 1989.
- 'Concrete masonry for the designer', BCA. ➔

BS 6073:Part 1 specifies a minimum average crushing strength of 2.8 N/mm² for concrete blocks 75 mm thick or greater. Blocks less than 75 mm thick are classed as nonloadbearing.

Concrete blocks are not suitable as damp proof courses or in foul drainage manholes. For guidance on use in other situations see BS 5628:Part 3, table 13. They should not be used in contact with ground from which there is danger of sulphate attack unless the units are protected or have been specifically selected for this purpose, i.e. made with sulphate resisting cement and/or with a certain minimum cement content – see BRE Digest 250.

7 SPECIAL SHAPES – BRICKS

BS 4729 specifies the dimensions of 'standard' special bricks. Many manufacturers will also make other shapes to order, but these may be limited by the manufacturing process and the nature of the material.

BS 4729 includes brick slips as special shapes. They should be manufactured with a keyed back to ensure a mechanical bond with the mortar.

Special shapes used as a feature requiring different mortar or jointing to the main walling, e.g. sills and parapet cappings, should be specified as a separate type of brickwork to draw attention to the differences.

BS 4729 notes that '. . . clay and calcium silicate bricks of special shapes and sizes may have a lower compressive strength than bricks made to BS 3921 and BS 187 from the same raw materials.' If compressive strength is critical, e.g. under the ends of lintels it may be advisable to have sample specials tested and to complete the design taking account of the results.

Insert, e.g.
45° external and internal angles as BS 4729.
To BS 4729, type as shown on drawings.
As detailed on drawing number FC(2)1–7.

8 SPECIAL SHAPES – BLOCKS

There is no British Standard for special shapes of blocks and therefore availability must be checked with manufacturers. As with bricks, purpose designed blocks and matching components can be produced. The special blocks required should be listed, e.g.

Half sizes	Corner blocks
Reveal blocks	Horizontal duct blocks
Half reveal blocks	Pier blocks
Coursing bricks	Lintels
Return blocks	Lintel trough blocks.

9 MORTAR

The basic ingredients and making of mortar generally are specified in section Z21. Mortar mixes for brickwork and blockwork may be specified in the types of walling clauses at the beginning of the section, by stating the constituents and proportions, e.g.
1:1:6 cement:lime:sand
1:5–6 white cement:selected white sand.

For guidance on selection of mortars for use in various situations see BS 5628:Part 3, table 13 or BRE Digest 160. In general, stronger bricks and blocks and more severe exposure conditions require mortars of higher strength, i.e. with a greater cement content. The weaker the mortar, the more will it accommodate small movements in the brickwork or blockwork, this being more critical in blockwork because there are fewer joints. Richer mortars are desirable for use with exposed bricks that contain appreciable quantities of

soluble sulphates (See BRE Digest 89 and Defect Action Sheet 128).

Brick sills and cappings are particularly vulnerable to frost action and a stronger mortar is required. It is preferable to joint the sills and cappings as the work proceeds rather than pointing separately. Sills and cappings should be specified as a separate type of brickwork to draw attention to the requirement for stronger mortar.

10 SPECIAL COLOUR OF MORTAR

When coloured mortar is required, it is better to specify coloured ready mixed material. Site mixing using pigments is rarely satisfactory, adequate control of colour consistency being very difficult. Remember that the colour of mortar changes whilst drying and setting. Insert, e.g.
Mortaco Ltd. brown reference BR44.
Red, using ready-mixed lime:sand and subject to approval of sample panel.
If mortar is not required to be coloured, delete the item.

11 BOND

Use the following terminology:

Half lap stretcher	*Flemish*
Third lap stretcher	*Flemish garden wall*
English	*Heading*
English garden wall	*Honeycomb*

12 JOINTS

This item applies only to facework including fair face work. Wall faces which are to be plastered or which will not be visible in the finished work are covered by relevant clauses in BS 8000:Part 3.

Insert details of joint profile and method of execution, e.g.
Flush pointed as clause 860. Profiles may be specified as:
Flush
Weathered
Bucket handle
Recessed square
Approved.

13 FEATURES

Insert brief details of any unusual requirements, cross referring where appropriate to sections F21, F30 and F31 and/or drawings, e.g.
Reinforcement over openings as section F30.
Brick corbelling to support joists.
Soldier course over openings.
Ashlar stone dressings as section F32.
Internal walls on suspended slabs reinforced in every bed joint as section F30.
Round windows formed with tapered blocks.

GUIDANCE NOTES

SPECIFICATION CLAUSES

F10   BRICK/BLOCK WALLING
To be read with Preliminaries/General conditions.

TYPES OF WALLING
See general guidance for advice on completing
clauses 110 to 390.

TYPE(S) OF WALLING

110   CLAY FACING BRICKWORK *EXTERNALLY* :
   • Bricks: To BS 3921.
     Manufacturer and reference: *Smith's Bricks, Russet*
     ~~Special shapes:~~ . . . .
   • Mortar: As section Z21.
     Mix: *1:1:6 cement* : *lime* : *sand*
     ~~Special colour:~~ . . . .
   • Bond: *Stretching*
   • Joints: *Flush* . .
   • Features: *Soldier course to parapet*

~~170~~ CALCIUM SILICATE FACING BRICKWORK . . . .
   • Bricks: To BS 187, Class . . . . . .
     Manufacturer and reference: . . . .
     Special shapes: . . . .
   • Mortar: As section Z21.
     Mix: . . . .
     Special colour: . . . .
   • Bond: . . . .
   • Joints: . . . .
   • Features: . . . .

~~210~~ CONCRETE FACING BRICKWORK . . . .
   • Bricks: To BS 6073:Part 1.
     Manufacturer and reference: . . . .
     Minimum average compressive strength: . . . . . . N/mm^2
     Work size(s): . . . .
     Special shapes: . . . .
   • Mortar: As section Z21.
     Mix: . . . .
     Special colour: . . . .
   • Bond: . . . .
   • Joints: . . . .
   • Features: . . . .

230
For advice on the use of second hand bricks see
'Salvage and reuse of bricks', Architects' Journal.

~~230~~ SECOND HAND FACING BRICKWORK . . . .
   • Bricks: Second hand bricks free from deleterious matter
     such as mortar, plaster, paint, bituminous materials and
     organic growths. Bricks to be sound, clean and reasonably
     free from cracks and chipped arrisses.
     Supplier/source: . . . .
   • Mortar: As section Z21.
     Mix: . . . .
     Special colour: . . . .
   • Bond: . . . .
   • Joints: . . . .
   • Features: . . . .

250

Blocks: Insert type of concrete, e.g.
Dense aggregate.
Aerated.
Work size(s): Specify face dimensions and the range of thicknesses required, e.g. *440 x 215 x 100, 140 and 190 mm.*
Finish/colour: Insert, e.g.
Shot blasted white.
Riven.
Exposed limestone aggregate.
Fluted charcoal.

290

This clause is for proprietary blocks which simulate natural stone rubble walling and normally form the outer leaf of a cavity wall. This type of reconstructed stonework is really only a variant of concrete blockwork and is quite distinct from simulated ashlar work.
Walling type: Insert, e.g.
Squared random rubble.
Rough hewn brought to courses.
Ashlar coursed and bonded as shown on drawings.
Finish/colour: Insert, e.g. *Weathered York.*
Special shapes: These include jumper blocks (to break up regular coursing), quoins, battered blocks, end blocks, capping blocks, sills, lintels, etc.
Mortar: See general guidance 9. Recommendations are normally the same as for concrete blockwork, but check with manufacturer.
Joints: Flush or concave (bucket handle) joints are usually the most suitable. Raked joints should not be used.
Features: Insert brief details of any unusual requirements, cross referring where appropriate to sections F30 and F31 and/or drawings, e.g.
Cast stone dressings as section F30.
Red brick quoins to corners and around openings, brickwork type F10/110.

310–340

Common brickwork is that which is not normally intended to be seen. If a brick marketed as a common is to be used as a facing or in fair faced work, specify in the appropriate facing brickwork clause.

310

Water absorption: This need only be specified if a characteristic flexural strength has been assumed for the design of common brickwork to resist bending due to lateral loads. Insert *Less than 7%* or *Between 7% and 12%'* or delete the item if greater than 12% is acceptable. See BS 5628:Part 1, table 3.

(250) CONCRETE FACING BLOCKWORK INTERNALLY :
- Blocks: *Dense aggregate* to BS 6073:Part 1.
  Manufacturer and reference: *Fortihall Settle White*
  ~~Minimum average compressive strength: ...... N/mm²~~
  Work size(s): *440 x 225 x 100 and 140 mm*
  Finish/~~colour~~: *Smooth or shot blasted (drawing 101)*
  ~~Special shapes:~~ ....
- Mortar: As section Z21.
  Mix: *1:1:6 cement : lime : sand*
  ~~Special colour:~~ ....
- Bond: *Stretching half lap*
- Joints: *Bucket handle*
- Features: *Reinforced block lintels*

~~**299**~~ RECONSTRUCTED STONEWORK ....
- Walling type: ....
  Manufacturer and reference: ....
  Finish/colour: ....
  Special shapes: ....
- Mortar: As section Z21.
  Mix: ....
  Special colour: ....
- Bond: ....
- Joints: ....
- Features: ....

~~**310**~~ CLAY COMMON BRICKWORK ....
- Bricks: To BS 3921.
  Minimum average compressive strength: ...... N/mm²
  Durability designation: ......
  Water absorption: ....
- Mortar: As section Z21.
  Mix: ....
- Bond: ....

~~**330**~~ CALCIUM SILICATE COMMON BRICKWORK ....
- Bricks: To BS 187, Class ......
- Mortar: As section Z21.
  Mix: ....
- Bond: ....

~~340~~ CONCRETE COMMON BRICKWORK . . . .
- Bricks: To BS 6073:Part 1.
  Minimum average compressive strength: . . . . . . N/mm²
  Work size(s): . . . .
- Mortar: As section Z21.
  Mix: . . . .
- Bond: . . . .

350
Common blockwork is that which is not normally intended to be seen. If a block marketed as a common is to be used as a facing or in fair faced work, specify in clause 250.
Blocks: Insert type of concrete, e.g. *Dense aggregate, Lightweight aggregate, Aerated.*
Thermal resistance: Thermal resistance need not be specified if blocks are not to be used as insulation, nor if a particular proprietary block is specified.

If the blocks are to be used, e.g. in the external leaf with a rendered coating, the thermal resistance should be specified at a moisture content of 5%. Amend the clause accordingly.
Work size(s): Specify face dimensions and the range of thickness required, e.g. 440 x 215 x 100, 140 and 190 mm.

(350) CONCRETE COMMON BLOCKWORK **BELOW DPC :**
- Blocks: **Dense aggregate** to BS 6073:Part 1.
  Manufacturer and reference: **Fortihall**
  Minimum average compressive strength: **20** . N/mm²
  ~~Thermal resistance: Not less than . . . . . . m² °C/W at 3%~~
  ~~moisture content.~~
  Work size(s): **440 x 215 x 100 and 140 mm**
  ~~Special shapes:~~ . . . .
- Mortar: As section Z21.
  Mix: **1 : ¼ : 3 sulphate resisting cement : lime : sand**
- Bond: **Stretching**

380
If engineering bricks are to be used as facings they should be specified in clause 110. There are two classes of engineering brick specified in BS 3921:
A Compressive strength not less than 70 N/mm² and water absorption not more than 4.5% by mass.
B Compressive strength not less than 50 N/mm² and water absorption not more than 7% by mass.

(380) ENGINEERING BRICKWORK **FOR MANHOLES :**
- Bricks: To BS 3921, Engineering Class **B** . . .
- Mortar: As section Z21.
  Mix: **1 : ¼ : 3 sulphate resisting cement : lime : sand**
- Bond: **English**
- Joints: Flush.

390
Two classes are specified in BS 3921:
1 Water absorption not more than 4.5% by mass.
2 Water absorption not more than 7% by mass.

Specify dpc bricks for freestanding boundary and garden walls rather than other dpc materials to ensure full bond strength – see Defect Action Sheets 129 and 130.

~~390~~ DAMP PROOF COURSE BRICKWORK:
- Bricks: To BS 3921, Damp proof course Class . . . . . .
  Manufacturer and reference: . . . .
- Mortar: As section Z21.
  Mix: . . . .
  Special colour: . . . .
- Bond: . . . .
- Joints: . . . .

WORKMANSHIP GENERALLY

410
Delete either section if not included in the project specification. Insert any of the following if included in the project specification:
F20 Natural stone rubble walling
F21 Natural stone ashlar walling/dressings.

(410) RELATED WORK is specified in the following sections:
F30 Accessories/Sundry items for brick/block/stone walling.
F31 Precast concrete sills/lintels/copings/features.

(421) BASIC WORKMANSHIP: Comply with the clauses of BS 8000:Part 3 which are relevant to this section.

(431) ACCURACY: Notwithstanding BS 8000:Part 3, clause 3.1.2, comply with Preliminaries clause A33/340 and any required critical dimensions given in the specification or on the drawings.

540, 541
Alternative clauses.

(540) COURSING: Gauge brick courses four to 300 mm including joints.

~~541~~ COURSING: Arrange brick courses to line up with existing work.

~~590~~ SUPPORT OF EXISTING WORK: Where new lintels or walling are to support existing structure, completely fill top joint with semidry mortar, hard packed and well rammed to ensure full load transfer after removal of temporary supports.

600
Insert appropriate details, e.g.
where shown on drawings.
unless specified otherwise.

~~600~~ BLOCK BOND new walls to existing, ... by cutting pockets into existing walls, not less than 100 mm deep, the full thickness of the new wall, and vertically as follows:
Brick to brick: 4 courses high at 8 course centres.
Brick to block, block to brick or block to block: Every alternate block course.
Bond new walling into pockets with all voids filled solid with mortar.

640
Sealing around pipes and ducts is covered by section P31.

~~640~~ FIRE STOPPING: Fill joints around joist ends built into cavity walls with mortar to seal cavities from interior of building.

641
Use for brick cladding to timber frame construction.

~~641~~ FIRE STOPPING: Ensure a tight fit between brickwork and cavity barriers to prevent fire and smoke penetration.

(660) HOLES, RECESSES AND CHASES IN BRICK/BLOCK WALLING: Comply with the relevant clause in section P31.

ADDITIONAL REQUIREMENTS FOR FACEWORK

740
BS 3921, Appendix F gives guidance on the visual assessment of facing bricks using panels of brickwork. The panels should be located in good natural light and, if possible, so that they can be seen in conjunction with the finished work. A viewing distance of 3 m will normally be satisfactory.
Walling type: Insert clause number.
Size of panel: 1.5 x 1.5 m is normal.
Including example of . . . Any features which are to be included in the sample should be listed, e.g.
soldier course.
brick on edge coping.
cut bricks at reveals.

(740) REFERENCE PANEL(S): Prepare panel(s) as set out below and, after drying out, obtain approval of appearance before proceeding. Construct panels in an approved location using randomly sampled bricks/blocks but rejecting any which are damaged.
- Walling type F10/ *110*
  Size of panel: . *2 m²*. . .
  Including example of *soldier course*
- Walling type F10/ *250*
  Size of panel: . *4 m²*. .
  Including example of . *lintel and control joint*

750
Manufacturers can help to overcome the problem of uneven colour distribution in several ways:
- Mixing bricks from different parts of the kiln before packaging.
- Reserving the whole of a kiln batch for the project when bricks are to be supplied over a long period.
- Mixing different kiln batches for very large projects.

(750) COLOUR MIXING:
- Agree with manufacturer and CA methods for ensuring that the supply of facing bricks/blocks is of a consistent, even colour range, batch to batch and within batches.
- Check each delivery for consistency of appearance with previous deliveries and do not use if variation is excessive.
- Mix different packs and deliveries which vary in colour to avoid patches, horizontal stripes and racking back marks in the finished work.

(760) APPEARANCE:
- Select bricks/blocks with unchipped arrises. Cut with a masonry saw where cut edges will be exposed to view.
- Set out and lay bricks to match appearance of relevant approved reference panel(s).
- Keep courses evenly spaced using gauge rods. Set out carefully to ensure satisfactory junctions and joints with adjoining or built-in elements and components.
- Protect facework against damage and disfigurement during the course of the works, particularly arrises of openings and corners.

790
Putlog holes are made good as the scaffolding is taken down. This can be detrimental to the appearance of the wall if mortar colour or workmanship in pointing are markedly different. The alternative is to use independent scaffolding which will increase the cost of the job. Therefore use this clause only when very high quality facing work is required.

860, 870, 880
See BRE Digest 200 and BS 6270:Part 1. Repairs should not be attempted unless movement has ceased. If cracked joints are not causing leakage, the decision to repoint will depend on visual considerations – cracks of 1.5 mm or less may be preferable to partial repointing. Rebedding should normally be done using a 1:1:6 mortar.
   Mortar for repointing must not be very different in strength to the existing mortar. As a general guide:

Existing mortar	Mortar for repointing
Strong	1:1:6
Normal	1:2:9
Weak	1:3:12

State if coloured mortar is required. See BDA Practical Note 7 and BS 6270: Part 1, clause 13.

 GROUND LEVEL: Facework to start not less than 150 mm below finished level of external paving or soil except where shown otherwise.

 PUTLOG SCAFFOLDING to facework will not be permitted.

800 **TOOTHED BOND:** Except where a straight vertical joint is specified, new and existing facework in the same plane to be bonded together at every course to give a continuous appearance.

820 **BRICK SILLS/CAPPINGS:** Bed solidly in mortar with vertical joints completely filled. Press mortar firmly into exposed joints and finish neatly.

860 **CRACKED BRICKS** in existing facework to be cut out and replaced with matching bricks bedded in . . . . cement: lime:sand . . . . mortar, before repointing adjacent cracked joints as specified.

870 **CRACKED JOINTS** in existing facework which is not to be repointed: joints with cracks wider than . . . . . . mm to be cut out to form a square recess of 15–20 mm depth. Remove dust, lightly wet and neatly point in . . . . cement: lime:sand mortar to match existing work.

880 **REPOINTING:** Where specified carefully rake out existing joints by hand to form a square recess of 15–20 mm depth. Remove dust, lightly wet and neatly point in . . . . cement:lime: sand mortar to a . . . . profile in a continuous operation.

5 Specification work sections

The previous chapters have covered the general principles of specification writing, this chapter deals with the actual preparation of a specification. Each Common Arrangement work section from A–Z is listed and each list (with the exception of A Preliminaries) opens with the full list of Common Arrangement headings. Under each section is set out a selection of elements likely to be encountered in domestic work or work of a simple nature, the selected elements each being marked with an asterisk and a selection of matters requiring specification is given. No such list can be comprehensive but the selections made are intended as a general guide. The CAWS headings not covered are, in the main, specialist work requiring a more detailed specification outside the scope of this book. It does not follow that each point mentioned should correspond with a clause in the specification: it may need several clauses or may be altogether unnecessary. It is obvious, for instance, that 'materials and workmanship' clauses of concrete will be much fuller for a reinforced concrete building than for a small house of traditional construction; or in a job where there are no suspended concrete floors the relative clauses will be omitted. The lists are lists of headings, and the writer should take each in turn asking 'Does this apply?' If it does, the next question is: 'What do I want?' When the section or part of the section has been completed the final question must not be forgotten: 'What else is wanted that is not on this list?'

Reference is given, where possible, to relative British Standards and Codes of Practice published by the British Standards Institution. The year reference is not quoted here, as these documents are revised from time to time: then the year reference is altered but the classification number normally remains the same. Up-to-date information as to currency of these standards and codes of practice will be found in the latest list (BSI Standards Catalogue – BSI) or can be ascertained by enquiry from the BSI. In addition to the sectional list there are available in four loose-leaf volumes summaries of British Standards for Building (BS Handbook 3 – BSI) to which addendum packets are issued from time to time on a subscription basis.

A   PRELIMINARIES/GENERAL CONDITIONS

Note: The JCT Standard Form of Contract is assumed and its Conditions
are not repeated here. If any other form is used, it should be checked
with the Standard Conditions and any clauses found missing should
be dealt with in the specification added to the conditions of contract.

A10	Project particulars	Position of the site Access for inspection, keys etc. Names and addresses: employer consultants
A11	Drawings	Schedule of drawings
A12	The site/Existing buildings	Site boundaries Existing buildings on site Existing buildings adjacent to site Existing services under and over the ground Trial hole information
A13	Description of the work	Brief description Details of work by others
A20	The Contract/Sub-contract	See note above Define the form Completion of blanks Amplifications or amendments Employer's insurance responsibilities Performance bonds Under hand or under deed

A30–A37 of the Common Arrangement cover the employer's requirements,
that is to say matters at the discretion of the employer which must be made
known to the contractor. It is therefore important that the employer's wishes
are known and if necessary advice will need to be given. Each project must
be treated on its merits but the following list, extracted in the main from
SMM7 gives a guide. To this list would need to be added other matters
special to the project, hence 'others – details stated'.

A30	Tendering/Sub-letting/Supply	Tender requirements Restrictions on sub-letting Purchase of materials
A31	Provision, content and use of documents	Extra drawings Operating manuals

A32	Management of the Works	Site agent Site meetings Instructions Programmes, records etc.
A33	Quality standards/control	Samples Testing Certificates British Standards/Codes of Practice Clerk of works
A34	Security/Safety/Protection	Noise and pollution control Maintain adjoining buildings Maintain public and private roads Maintain live services Security Protection of work in all sections Others – details stated
A35	Specific limitations on method/sequence/timing	Design constraints Limitations, restrictions etc. Others – details stated

A36	Employer's requirements for
	facilities/temporary
	works/services
		Accommodation
		   temporary fences, hoardings, screens
		   and roofs
		Name boards
		Technical and surveying equipment
		Temperature and humidity
		Telephone/Facsimile installation and
		   rental/maintenance
		Others – details stated

A37	Operation/Maintenance of the finished building	

A40–A44 of the Common Arrangement cover the contractor's general cost items. Here the items are just listed for the convenience of the contractor in pricing. No details can be given as these are matters for the contractor to decide upon, hence 'others' is solely a reminder for the contractor to think of anything else he needs to price. The only exception to this is where the employer intends to make facilities available, such as space for messrooms, water and power for the works etc. In these cases details do need to be given.

A40	Management and staff	Contractor to decide
A41	Site accommodation	This is for the contractor to decide. If space etc is being made available details must be stated setting out any restrictions on use, leaving clean etc.

A42	Services and facilities	Power
		Lighting
		Fuels
		Water
		Telephones and administration
		Safety, health, and welfare
		Storage of materials
		Rubbish disposal
		Cleaning
		Drying out
		Protection of work in all sections
		Security
		Maintain private and public roads
		Small plant and tools
		General attendance on nominated sub-contractors
		Others
A43	Mechanical plant	Cranes
		Hoists
		Personnel transport
		Earthmoving plant
		Concrete plant
		Piling plant
		Paving and surfacing plant
		Others
A44	Temporary works	Temporary roads
		Temporary walkways
		Access scaffolding
		Support scaffolding and propping
		Hoardings, fans, fencing etc.
		Hardstanding
		Traffic regulations
		Others

A50–A55 of the Common Arrangement cover the remaining general items under this section.

A50	Work/Materials by the Employer	Work by others directly employed by the employer – details stated
		Attendance on others directly employed by the employer – details stated
		Materials provided by the employer – details stated
A51	Nominated sub-contractors	Add to PC sums for:
		profit
		unloading and storing materials

A51   Nominated sub-contractors   distributing materials in the building
       continued   returning empties
                                          supplying water
                                          allowing use of plant or fixed
                                              scaffolding
                                          any special scaffolding
                                          general attendance
                                          cleaning up
                                          examine specialists' estimates for any
                                              special conditions

A52   Nominated suppliers   Add to PC sums for:
                                          profit
                                          carriage to site
                                          unloading and storing
                                          fixing as described
                                          returning empties carriage paid

A53   Work by statutory authorities   Provisional sums for:
                                          Crossings to public footways
                                          Sewer connections
                                          Water mains
                                          Gas and/or electric mains
                                          Building control fees etc.
                                          Hoardings
                                          Tests of materials

A54   Provisional work   Provisional sums how adjusted
                                          Contingency provision

A55   Dayworks   Any restrictions on daywork
                                          Information required
                                          Provision for daywork

B   COMPLETE BUILDINGS

B1   Proprietary buildings   B10   Proprietary buildings*

Specification of proprietary buildings is a matter for detailed reference to the chosen supplier's technical information giving as much or as little detail as is required to adequately price, purchase and subsequently erect the building or buildings. The infra-structure required to accommodate such buildings would be specified either as a section on its own or as part of a main specification.

C DEMOLITION/ALTERATION/RENOVATION

C1　Demolition

C2　Alteration – composite items

C3　Alteration – support

C4　Repairing/Renovating
　　　concrete/masonry

C5　Repairing/Renovating
　　　metal/timber

C10　Demolishing structures*

C20　Alterations – spot items*

C30　Shoring

C40　Repairing/Renovating
　　　concrete/brick/block/stone

C41　Chemical dpcs to existing walls

C50　Repairing/Renovating metal

C51　Repairing/Renovating timber

C52　Fungus/Beetle eradication

Note: This section of the specification covers those works for which the estimator will require to see the site. In the case of a new building and a clear site there may be nothing at all, or perhaps only some openings in fence or hedge.

C1　Demolition

C10　Demolishing structures

Demolition	Describe extent with reference to drawings Grubbing up or sealing off drains and services Felling of trees (identified on drawing) and general clearance of site
Clearing site	Clearing site of rubbish, debris, overgrowth, etc.
Boundaries of site	Alterations (e.g. openings through or moving of fences, etc.): each boundary in turn
Temporary cross-overs	Temporary cross-overs to public footpath for access to the works
Obstructions	Provisional sums for moving lamp posts, telephone poles, etc.
Disposal of old materials	State if reserved for employer, otherwise clearing away will imply that they become the contractors' property and they will allow credit accordingly

Removal of toxic materials   State if the presence of materials such as
                                    asbestos lagging is known or suspected to
                                    exist, including indicating any special
                                    measures and/or restrictions as to their
                                    removal

C2   Alteration – composite items

C20 Alterations – spot items

Alterations   Alterations in buildings, taken, so far as
                                    practicable, room by room. Systematic and
                                    consistent order in each room, e.g.:
                                        Ceiling
                                        Walls
                                        Floors
                                        Windows
                                        Doors
                                        Fittings
                                    Define in a preamble the full meaning of such
                                    short descriptions as may be constantly
                                    repeated, e.g. 'overhaul window', 'overhaul
                                    lock', 'make good plaster', etc.

D GROUNDWORK

D1	Ground investigation/ stabilisation/dewatering	D10	Ground investigation
		D11	Soil stabilisation
		D12	Site dewatering
D2	Excavation/Filling	D20	Excavating and filling*
D3	Piling	D30	Cast in place concrete piling
		D31	Preformed concrete piling
		D32	Steel piling
D4	Diaphragm walling	D40	Diaphragm walling
D5	Underpinning	D50	Underpinning*

BS 8000   : Workmanship on building sites
  (Part 1)   : Excavation and filling – D20

D2   Excavation/filling

D20 Excavating and filling

BS 8004	: Code of practice for foundations
Surface soil	Stripping any turf, rolling and stacking Stripping surface soil and vegetable matter
Reducing levels	Any further surface excavation necessary
Basement	Excavation for basement
Trenches	Excavation for wall foundations, stanchion bases, etc. Define the depths to be estimated for if not shown on drawings. 'Depth required' is not good enough for pricing
Consolidation	Trimming and consolidating ground under concrete or hardcore
Excess excavation	Excess excavation (e.g., dug too deep) to be filled with concrete
Disposal	Disposal of excavated material – (a) vegetable soil; (b) general material; including filling and compacting around foundations and under floors; where disposed of on site, position of dumps to be defined as accurately as possible. (Where material is removed from the site the tip is a matter for the contractor)

	Temporary dumps for vegetable soil reserved for flower beds, etc. (See Q30 and 31)
	Material to be reserved for making up levels around building on completion and any forming of banks, etc. (See Q30 and 31)
Earth support	Provide all necessary earth support
Pumping etc.	Keep excavations, basements, ducts, etc., free from water
Filling	Material to be used
	Maximum thickness of layers and method of consolidation
	Extent and thicknesses (after consolidation) of beds
	Blinding top surface to receive concrete
	Any finishing to falls

D5   Underpinning

D50 Underpinning

Underpinning	Define nature and extent of underpinning and limit of length to be carried out in one operation
	Contractor to allow for necessary shoring
	Cutting away of old concrete or brick footings and excavation

E IN SITU CONCRETE/LARGE PRECAST CONCRETE

E1	In situ concrete	E10	In situ concrete*
		E11	Gun applied concrete
E2	Formwork	E20	Formwork for in situ concrete*
E3	Reinforcement	E30	Reinforcement for in situ concrete*
		E31	Post tensioned reinforcement for in situ concrete
E4	In situ concrete sundries	E40	Designed joints in in situ concrete*
		E41	Worked finishes/Cutting to in situ concrete*
		E42	Accessories cast into in situ concrete*
E5	Precast concrete large units	E50	Precast concrete large units*
E6	Composite construction	E60	Precast/Composite concrete decking

BS 8000   : Workmanship on building sites
  (Part 2.1) : Mixing and transporting concrete – E10
  (Part 2.2) : Placing, compaction and curing – E10

E1 In situ concrete

E10 In situ concrete

Materials and Workmanship

BS 12	: Portland cement
812	: Testing aggregates
877	: Foamed slag
882	: Aggregates
915	: High alumina cement
1047	: Air-cooled blast furnace aggregate
1165	: Clinker aggregate
1199–1200	: Building sands
1521	: Building paper

Cement
Fine aggregate (sand)
Coarse aggregate:
  general concrete
  fine concrete
  any special
Waterproofing compound
Water
Composition of mixes with note of
  abbreviated references (e.g. 1:2:4)
Method of mixing (hand and machine)
Frost and temperature control
Depositing, including minimum cover
  to reinforcement

1881	: Testing concrete	Compacting, vibrating etc.
3148	: Tests for water	Protection and curing
3681	: Sampling and testing of lightweight aggregates	Tests of individual materials
		Tests of concrete cubes
		Loading tests on finished work
		Building paper or polythene sheeting under concrete
3797	: Lightweight aggregates	
4016	: Building paper (breather type)	
4027	: Sulphate resisting Portland cement	
5075	: Concrete admixtures	
5328	: Methods of specifying concrete including ready mixed concrete	
5835	: Testing aggregates	
5950 (Part 3)	: Design in composite construction	
8102	: Code of Practice for protection of structures against water from the ground	
8110	: Structural use of concrete	
CP 102	: Protection from ground water	

Mass concrete foundations	Mix
BS 8004	: Code of practice for foundations	Widths and thicknesses (or reference to drawings if there shown)
		Laps at steps
		Any sloping tops, etc.

Mass concrete beds	Mix
Reinforced foundations and beds	Thickness
Suspended slabs	Construction joints
Walls	Any preparatory wrapping of steel joists
Column and stanchion casings	Compacting or vibrating
Beam and beam casings	
Staircases	

E2   Formwork

E20 Formwork for in situ concrete

Materials and workmanship
  BS 3809   : Wood wool
              permanent
              formwork and
              infill units

Formwork:
  Strength
  Hardboard lining, etc.
  Retarding liquid
  Time for removal
  Finish from wrot formwork
  Splays, chamfers, etc.
  Mortices, boxings, etc.

E3   Reinforcement

E30 Reinforcement for in situ concrete

Materials and workmanship
  BS 4449   : Steel bars

     4466   : Bending
                dimensions of
                bars
    4482–3 : Steel fabric
     4486   : H.T. bars for pre-
                stressed concrete
     5896   : Steel wire for pre-
                stressed concrete
     6722   : Recommendations
                for dimensions

Reinforcement:
  Steel bars
  Steel wire, fabric, giving laps, etc.
Hooked ends to bars, cranking, placing,
  tying wire, etc.

Reinforced foundations and beds
Suspended slabs
Walls
Columns and stanchion casings
Beam and beam casings
Staircases

Reinforcement (e.g. reference number of
wire fabric or reference to drawings or
schedule of bars)

E4   In situ concrete sundries

E40 Designed joints in in situ concrete

Expansion and contraction joints
   BS 6093   : Code of practice
                        Design of joints
                           and jointing in
                           building
                           construction
	Type of joint

E41 Worked finishes/Cutting to in situ concrete

Preparation of concrete for key for
   plaster etc.
Description and extent of any worked
   finish to concrete surface
Floor channels etc.
Grouting to holes, bolts, stanchion
   bases, etc.
Surface hardeners

E42 Accessories cast into in situ concrete

Provision for holding down bolts
Fixing strips and anchors
Insert plugs
Ties

E5   Precast concrete large units

E50   Precast concrete large units

Hollow tile or pre-cast slab floors and roofs (for estimating by specialists)

Superimposed load per square metre which is to be assumed
  (a) for floors (any floors taking special loads, e.g. safes, tanks, etc., mentioned with the loads to be reckoned)
  (b) for roofs

Drawings supplied showing extent of the work

Any supporting beams, beam casings, etc., required to be included shown marked on drawings

Minimum bearings (end and side)

Specialist to supply specification of his system

Conditions of sub-contract including cash discount to be included

Note: If the floors or roofs have been designed in detail, they can be specified as described above for suspended slabs or pre-cast work, with the addition of the description of hollow tiles or other special units

F MASONRY

F1   Brick/Block walling

F2   Stone walling

F3   Masonry accessories

F10   Brick/Block walling*
F11   Glass block walling*

F20   Natural stone rubble walling*
F21   Natural stone/ashlar walling/
          dressings*
F22   Cast stone walling/dressings*

F30   Accessories/sundry items for
          brick/block/stone walling*
F31   Precast concrete sills/lintels/
          copings/features*

BS 8000   : Workmanship on building sites
   (Part 3)   : Masonry – F10, F30

F1   Brick/Block walling

F10 Brick/Block walling

Materials and workmanship
   BS 12   : Portland cement
      187   : Calcium silicate
                           bricks
      890   : Limes
   1199–1200 : Sand
      3921   : Clay bricks
      4551   : Testing mortars
      4721   : Ready-mixed lime
                           sand for mortar
      4729   : Special bricks
      4887   : Mortar admixtures
      5628   : Structural
                           recommendations
      6073   : Precast masonry
                           units
      6649   : Clay and calcium
                           silicate modular
                           bricks
      8004 ⎫   : Code of practice
      8103 ⎭   for foundations

General bricks –
   (a) below damp-proof course
   (b) above damp-proof course
Facing bricks
Cement
Lime
Sand
Admixtures

Mortar composition and mixing –
   (a) cement mortar
   (b) lime or cement – lime mortar
   (c) any special pointing mortar
Bond of general brickwork
General workmanship in bricklaying
   (filling joints solid, keeping perpends,
   carrying up walls evenly, wetting
   bricks, protection against frost, etc.)
Pointing of fair face to common
   brickwork
Pointing of facing bricks

CP 102   : Protection from ground water

Gauge for height of courses (e.g. 13 courses to 1.00 m, assuming a metric brick 65 mm thick and a 10 mm joint)

Walls

Building of walls

Construction of hollow walls, giving width of cavity and spacing of ties

If generally lime or cement-lime mortar, state extent of work to be in cement mortar

Preparation of existing walls for raising

Any thickening of existing walls with extent of bonding to old

Wall finish (internal)

Extent of fair face. Refer to Schedule if any

Describe pointing and state if to be carried out as the work proceeds

Grooved bricks on surfaces to be plastered (if applicable)

Wall finish (external)

Extent of facing bricks

String courses, bands, quoins and other dressings

Block partitions and walling

    BS 6073   : Precast concrete masonry units

Make, thickness and surface finish

Mortar, erection and bonding

Bonding to brickwork

Pinning up top edges

Sundries and general labours

Rough and fair cutting

Raking out joints of brickwork (if necessary) as key for plastering, etc.

Raking out joints for asphalt damp-proof courses, skirtings, etc., and pointing top edge

Raking out joint for turn in of lead or copper flashings and pointing

Eaves filling

Fixing bricks

Cutting rebates, splays, chases, holes, etc.

Cutting and pinning ends of timbers, lintels, etc.

Cutting, toothing and bonding new walls to old

Pinning up top of walls to underside of steel joists (not bearing on them) or to existing soffites

Centring

F11 Glass block walling

Type and size of glass blocks
Mortar
Temporary works including formwork
  if required

F2   Stone walling

F20 Natural stone/rubble walling

Walling   Stone
  BS 5390   : Stone masonry   Mortar
                                                   Whether random rubble, coursed, etc.
                                                   Finish to exposed face (if in the same
                                                     stone)
                                                   Facing (if of a different stone) with
                                                     finish to face and spacing of bonders
                                                   Type of quoins, lintels, etc.
                                                   Coping
                                                   Centring

F21 Natural stone/ashlar walling/dressings

Dressings   To be set on natural bed
  BS 6477   : Water repellents   Finish to surface generally
    5642   : Sills and copings   Mortar for setting and pointing
                                                   Bonding to backing
                                                   Treatment to back, e.g. coating of lime
  CP 202   : Tile and slab   Coating face with slurry and cleaning
                             flooring   down
                                                   Protection
                                                   Extent of general stone facing and any
                                                     special descriptions or instructions
                                                   Where stonework is in dressings only,
                                                     give positions and sizes:
                                                         Plinth
                                                         String courses
                                                         Window and door surrounds
                                                         Cornices
                                                         Copings
                                                   Pavings, steps, etc.
                                                   Padstones
                                                   Casing up and protection
                                                   Centring

F22 Cast stone walling/dressings

BS 1217	: General		Paving: thickness, size of slabs and surface finish
3826, 6477	: Water repellents		
5642	: Sills and copings		Corbel courses: width and thickness
6457	: Reconstructed stone masonry units		Cover stones on girders: ditto
			Padstones under ends of beams: sizes and positions with surface finish to exposed faces
7263	: Flags, kerbs, channels, edgings and quadrants		Steps: sizes and positions
			Landings: ditto
			Hearths: ditto
CP 202	: Tile and slab flooring		Maker's name if a specialist's material is required
			Colour and texture
			Otherwise specify in the same way as a variety of natural stone

F3   Masonry Accessories

F30 Accessories/Sundry items for brick/block/stone walling

Proprietary sills, lintels, copings, windows boards, etc.		Type and size and proprietary reference
		Hoisting
		Bedding and pointing
		Temporary supports
Reinforcement		Expanded metal or proprietary brand
		Spacing of reinforcement in thickness and height of wall
Forming cavities		Width of cavity
BS 6676	: Thermal insulation of cavity walls	Rigid sheet insulation
Wall ties, anchors, cramps, dowels, etc.		Type size and spacing
BS 1243	: Wall ties	
Damp proof courses		General damp-proof course
BS 743	: Generally	Ditto to parapets
6398	: Bitumen	Ditto to chimney stacks
6515	: Polyethylene	Ditto over openings in hollow walls or where hollow walls are built solid
		Ditto to jambs of hollow walls
Flue linings, terminals		Fireplaces and their fixing
BS 41	: Cast iron flue pipes	Firebrick linings
567	: Asbestos cement flue pipes (light)	Chimney pots
		Brick hearths

835	: Asbestos cement flue pipes (heavy)
1181	: Clay flue linings and flue terminals
1289	: Flue blocks and masonry terminals for gas appliances
5440	: Flues
5854	: Code of Practice for flues and flue structures in buildings
6461	: Masonry chimneys
(Part 1)	and flue pipes
(Part 2)	: Factory made insulated chimneys for internal applications

Air bricks and gratings
BS 493   : Air bricks and
                   gratings

Type, size and location (check these are
   shown on drawings or specify the
   number required)
Flues through walls
Inside finish (cross-reference if in
   another section)

Fixing items

Cutting and pinning ends of timbers,
   lintels, etc.
Bedding plates, door frames, etc.
Building in metal windows, doors, etc.

F31 Pre-cast concrete sills/lintels/
copings/features (Non proprietary)

BS 5642	: Sills and copings	Mix
5977	: Lintels	Sizes of members
6073	: Masonry units	Reinforcement if any
7263	: Flags, kerbs, channels, edgings and quadrants	Surface finish
		Dowels
		Bedding and pointing
		Forming holes
		Hoisting
		Fixing slips, cramps, etc.
		Fixings
		Temporary supports

G　STRUCTURAL/CARCASSING METAL/TIMBER

G1　Structural/Carcassing metal　　　G10　Structural steel framing*
　　　　　　　　　　　　　　　　　　　G11　Structural aluminium framing
　　　　　　　　　　　　　　　　　　　G12　Isolated structural metal
　　　　　　　　　　　　　　　　　　　　　　members*

G2　Structural/Carcassing timber　　　G20　Carpentry/Timber framing/First
　　　　　　　　　　　　　　　　　　　　　　fixing*

G3　Metal/Timber decking　　　　　　　G30　Metal profiled sheet decking
　　　　　　　　　　　　　　　　　　　G31　Prefabricated timber unit decking
　　　　　　　　　　　　　　　　　　　G32　Edge supported/Reinforced
　　　　　　　　　　　　　　　　　　　　　　woodwool slab decking*

BS 8000　　　　: Workmanship on building sites
　(Part 5)　　　: Carpentry, joinery, general fixings – G20

G1　Structural/Carcassing metal

G10　Structural steel framing

Structural Steel
　BS 4　　　　: Hot-rolled sections
　　449　⎱
　　　　　　⎬ : Use of structural
　　5950 ⎰ 　　　steel in building
　　2994　　: Cold rolled steel
　　　　　　　　sections
　　3139　　: Bolts
　　4174　　: Self-tapping screws
　　4604　　: High strength
　　　　　　　　friction grip
　　　　　　　　bolts
　　4848　　: Hot-rolled
　　　　　　　　structural steel
　　　　　　　　sections

For simple construction fixed by the
　builder the sizes of members must be
　given according to the British
　Standard sections. It is important
　where the same size member is made
　with two different weights to specify
　the weight required, e.g. 203×133
　mm $\times$ 25 kg per m or 203×133 m $\times$
　30 kg per m beams
Cleated connections and their rivets and
　bolts
Holding down bolts
Reference to any padstones, etc.,
　specified elsewhere
In more elaborate construction the
　work will usually be entrusted to a
　specialist and a specification is a
　matter for a structural engineer

G12　Isolated structural metal members

Isolated members

Wall plates, bearing bars etc.
Isolated structural beams, columns, etc.

G2   Structural/Carcassing timber

G20   Carpentry/Timber framing/First fixing

Materials and workmanship

BS 144	: Creosote
589 }	. Nomenclature of
881 }	: ⎯ timber
1202	: Nails
1494	: Fixing accessories
1579	: Connectors for timber
4072	: Wood preservation
4169	: Laminated structural members
4471	: Sizes of sawn and processed softwood
4978	: Timber grades for structural use
5268	: Code of practice for structural use of timber
6100	: Glossary of terms
6178	: Joist hangers

Timber generally
Softwood
Hardwoods
Basic sizes given: allowances or finished
   sizes (sawn and wrot)
Spacing of structural timbers in timber
   floor, roof or partition construction
Trimming of ditto; extra thickness of
   trimming joists and trimmers
Metal connectors, straps, hangers, bolts,
   ties, etc. off site preservatives

Floors

Plates
Joists
Trimming
Strutting
Bridging pieces

Timber stud partitions

Heads
Sills
Studs
Braces
Noggings
Trimming

Pitched roofs

Plates
Rafters and collars
Ridge
Hips and dragon ties
Valleys
Purlins and their struts
Trusses
Sprockets and tilting fillets
Ceiling joists

	Binders and hangers to ditto
	Dormers
	Trimming
	Battens
	Roof boarding
	Walking boards in roof space
	Trap door to ditto
	Any special features, e.g. turrets
Eaves and verge finishes	Wrot ends to rafters
	Fascia
	Soffit and bearers (size and spacing)
	Bedmould
	Barge boards
	Parapet and other boxed gutters
	Snow boards
Grounds, bearers, firrings, etc	Wall battens: size, spacing and fixing
	Noggings for joints of plaster board or similar coverings: ditto. (Where not an integral part of linings or partitions system)
	Grounds for fibrous plaster work: ditto
	Firrings
Fixings	Bearers (e.g. for cisterns)
	Fixing slips in joints
	Plugging

G3   Metal/Timber decking

G32 Edge supported/Reinforced woodwool slab decking

Flat roofs	Decking
BS 1105	: Woodwool cement slabs	Supports and fixings
	Angle fillets for turn-up of felt roofing etc.

H   CLADDING/COVERING

H1	Glazed cladding/covering	H10	Patent glazing*	
		H11	Curtain walling	
		H12	Plastics glazed vaulting/walling	
		H13	Structural glass assemblies	
		H14	Concrete rooflights/pavement lights*	
H2	Sheet/Board cladding	H20	Rigid sheet cladding	
		H21	Timber weatherboarding	
H3	Profiled sheet cladding/ covering/siding	H30	Fibre cement profiled sheet cladding/covering/siding*	
		H31	Metal profiled/flat sheet cladding/covering/siding*	
		H32	Plastics profiled sheet cladding/ covering/siding*	
		H33	Bitumen and fibre profiled sheet cladding/covering*	
H4	Profiled panel cladding	H40	Glass reinforced cement cladding/features	
		H41	Glass reinforced plastics cladding/features	
H5	Slab cladding	H50	Precast concrete slab cladding/ features	
		H51	Natural stone slab cladding/ features	
		H52	Cast stone slab cladding/features	
H6	Slate/Tile cladding/covering	H60	Clay/Concrete roof tiling*	
		H61	Fibre cement slating*	
		H62	Natural slating*	
		H63	Reconstructed stone slating/ tiling*	
		H64	Timber shingling	
H7	Malleable sheet coverings/ cladding	H70	Malleable metal sheet prebonded coverings/cladding	
		H71	Lead sheet coverings/flashings*	
		H72	Aluminium sheet coverings/ flashings*	
		H73	Copper sheet coverings/ flashings*	
		H74	Zinc sheet coverings/flashings*	
		H75	Stainless steel coverings/ flashings*	

H76   Fibre bitumen thermoplastic
sheet coverings/flashings

BS 8000   : Workmanship on building sites
    (Part 5)   : Carpentry, joinery, general fixings – H21
    (Part 6)   : Slating and tiling of roofs and claddings – H60, H61, H62

H1   Glazed cladding/covering

H10 Patent glazing

Patent roof glazing   Type of glass
    BS 5516   : Code of practice for Type of bar, spacing and method of
                        patent glazing   fixing
                                            Clips to foot of glazing
                                            Finish to ridges, hips and valleys

H14 Concrete rooflights/pavement lights

Concrete rooflights and pavement   Maker and type (or PC sum)
    lights   Over-all sizes
                                            Size of lenses
                                            Method of fixing (with reference to kerb
                                                in Masonry)
                                            Any intermediate supports

H3   Profiled sheet cladding/covering/siding

H30 Fibre cement profiled sheet cladding/covering/siding
H31 Metal profiled/flat sheet cladding/covering/siding
H32 Plastics profiled sheet cladding/covering/siding
H33 Bitumen and fibre profiled sheet cladding/covering

Fibre cement sheet coverings   Material
    (for slating see under H61)   Type of sheet, e.g. standard corrugated
    BS 690   : Asbestos-cement   (small section), standard corrugated
                        sheets   (large section), reinforced corrugated
        1494   : Fixing accessories Side lap and end lap
        5247   : Sheet roof and wall Method of fixing (drive screws, clip
                        coverings   bolts and their washers)
                                            Ridge covering ⎤   If in lead,
                                            Hip ditto   ⎥   aluminium,
                                            Valley ditto   ⎬   copper or zinc
                                            Vertical angle ⎥   specify under
                                            covering   ⎦   H71–H74

Sheet metal coverings (other than flat
lead, zinc, aluminium or copper)

BS 1494	:	Fixing accessories
3083	:	Hot-dip zinc coated corrugated steel sheets
4154	:	Corrugated plastic translucent sheets
4842	:	Liquid coatings
4868	:	Profiled aluminium sheets
6496 } 6497 }	:	Powder coatings
CP 143 (Part 1)	:	Aluminium corrugated and troughed sheets
(Part 10)	:	Galvanised corrugated steel

Bitumen and fibre sheet

CP 143 (Part 16)	:	Semi-rigid asbestos bitumen sheet

H6   Slate/Tile cladding/covering

H60 Clay/Concrete roof tiling
H61 Fibre cement slating
H62 Natural slating
H63 Reconstructed stone slating/tiling

Tiling

			Type and size of tiles/slates
BS 402	:	Clay plain tiles	Lap
473	:	Concrete ditto	Nailing (any differences for steep slopes or vertical faces)
5534	:	Code of Practice	Double course to eaves

Verge (tile/slate-and-a-half width, undercloak and bedding)

Ridge covering ⎫ If in lead,
Hip ditto   ⎬ aluminium,
Valley ditto   ⎬ copper or zinc
Vertical angle ⎬ specify under
  covering   ⎭ H71–H74
Hip irons
Fixing lead soakers
Glass tiles or similar items

Slating
  BS 680   : Roofing slates
     690   : Asbestos cement
                  slates
    5534   : Code of Practice

Roofing felt
  BS 747   : Roofing felts   Underfelt to flat roofs
                                    Ditto to sloping roofs

H7   Malleable sheet coverings/cladding

H71 Lead sheet coverings/flashings

Sheet lead work   Flats
  BS 1178   : Milled lead sheet   Gutters and
                  for building   cesspools
                  purposes   Flashings and
     6915   : Lead roof and wall   aprons
                  coverings   Ridge, hip and   Thickness
                                         valley coverings   of lead and
                                       Dormer tops and   girths
                                         cheeks   where not
                                       Saddles, slates, etc.   defined on
                                       Soakers   drawings.
                                       Shoots into   Size and
                                         rainwater heads   spacing of
                                       Damp-proof   tacks.
                                         courses, aprons
                                         through cavity
                                         walls, to edges of
                                         asphalt, etc.
                                       Wedging flashings
                                       Bedding edges or turning into grooves,
                                         welting, etc.
                                       Soldered angles and seams
                                       Bossing to rolls, mouldings, etc.
                                       Copper nailing
                                       Timber rolls

H72 Aluminium sheet coverings/flashings
H73 Copper sheet coverings/flashings
H74 Zinc sheet coverings/flashings
H75 Stainless steel sheet coverings/flashings

Aluminium work (flat sheets: for
  corrugated sheeting see H31)

CP 143	: Aluminium roof
(Part 15)	and wall
	coverings

Copper work

BS 2870	: Sheet copper
CP 143	: Copper sheet roof
(Part 12)	and wall
	coverings

Zinc work

BS 849	: Zinc roofing
CP 143	: Zinc sheet roof and
(Part 5)	wall coverings

Sub-divided as for lead sheet coverings
  (H71)
Gauge
Method of jointing

J WATERPROOFING

J1 Cementitious coatings	J10 Specialist waterproof rendering
J2 Asphalt coatings	J20 Mastic asphalt tanking/damp proof membranes*
	J21 Mastic asphalt roofing/insulation/finishes*
	J22 Proprietary roof decking with asphalt finish
J3 Liquid applied coatings	J30 Liquid applied tanking/damp proof membranes
	J31 Liquid applied waterproof roof coatings
	J32 Sprayed vapour barriers
	J33 In situ glass reinforced plastics
J4 Felt/flexible sheets	J40 Flexible sheet tanking/damp proof membranes
	J41 Built up felt roof coverings*
	J42 Single layer plastics roof coverings
	J43 Proprietary roof decking with felt finish

BS 8000   : Workmanship on building sites
  (Part 4)   : Waterproofing – J20, J21, J30, J40, J41

J2   Asphalt coatings

J20 Mastic asphalt tanking/damp proof membranes

Tanking/Damp-proof courses		General damp-proof course (usually 2 coat)
BS 6577	: (natural rock)	Tanking (usually 3 coat)
6925	: (limestone aggregate)	Key of vertical into brick joints
		Angle fillets

J21 Mastic asphalt roofing/insulation/finishes

Roofing		Felt underlay
BS 747	: Felt	Flat roof (usually 2 coat)
6577	: (natural rock)	Vertical or sloping faces
6925	: (limestone aggregate)	Angle fillets
		Arrises and nosings

CP 144 (Part 4)	: Mastic asphalt	Skirtings: thickness, height and finish to top edge
Tile paving		Size and thickness of tiles (colour if coloured) Bedding material Joints: thickness and whether broken Skirtings: section

J4   Felt/flexible sheets

J41 Built up felt roof coverings

Felt roofing		Name of material, if a particular brand
BS 747	: Felt roofing	If single layer, type and weight per roll
CP 144 (Part 3)	: Roof coverings	If built-up roofing, number of layers and type and weight per roll of each layer Bedding composition Surface finish, e.g. gritting, insulating tiles, macadam, etc. Angle fillet Skirtings and turn-ups over angle fillet

K   LININGS/SHEATHING/DRY PARTITIONING

K1	Rigid sheet sheathing/linings	K10	Plasterboard dry lining*
		K11	Rigid sheet flooring/sheathing/ linings/casings*
		K12	Under purlin/Inside rail panel linings
		K13	Rigid sheet fine linings/ panelling*
K2	Board/Strip sheathing/linings	K20	Timber board flooring/ sheathing/linings/casings*
		K21	Timber narrow strip flooring/ linings
K3	Dry partitions/linings	K30	Demountable partitions
		K31	Plasterboard fixed partitions/ inner walls/linings*
		K32	Framed panel cubicle partitions
		K33	Concrete/Terrazzo partitions
K4	False ceilings/floors	K40	Suspended ceilings*
		K41	Raised access floors

BS 8000   : Workmanship on building sites
  (Part 5)   : Carpentry, joinery, general fixings – K11, K20
  (Part 8)   : Plasterboard partitions and dry linings – K10, K31

K1   Rigid sheet sheathing/linings

K10 Plasterboard dry lining

BS 1230	: Gypsum board	Type of board, thickness and method of
4022	: Gypsum wall board panels	fixing Scrimming of joints
6214	: Jointing materials	
6452	: Beads	
8212	: Code of practice for dry-lining using gypsum board	

K11 Rigid sheet flooring/sheathing/linings/casings

BS 1105	: Woodwool cement boards	Boarding: Make and thickness
3444	: Blockboard and laminboard	Method of fixing, nails, etc. Bearers
5669	: Chipboard	Cover fillets
6566	: Plywood	Pipe casings

K13 *Rigid sheet fine linings/panelling*

BS 3757	: Rigid PVC sheets	Type and thickness of material
3794	: Decorative high pressure laminates based on thermosetting resins	Bearers
		Treatment of joints
		Applied mouldings
		Mouldings formed on the solid
		Carving
		Fixings
4965	: Decorative panels	

K2   Board/Strip sheathing/linings

K20 *Timber board flooring/sheathing/linings/casings*

BS 8201	: Code of practice for timber flooring	Type and thickness of material
		Method of fixing
		Jointing
		Surface finish

K3   Dry partitioning/linings

K31 *Plasterboard fixed partitions/inner walls/linings*

BS 1230	: Gypsum board	Linings
4022	: Gypsum wall board panels	Studs, head and sole plates, etc.
		Insulation
5234	: Code of practice partitioning	Joint supports and treatment
		Intersection angles, abutments, etc.
6214	: Jointing materials	Cutting or fitting for doors and the like
6452	: Beads	Surface treatment
7364	: Galvanised steel studs and channels	
8212	: Code of practice for partitioning using gypsum board	

K4   False ceilings/floors

K40 *Suspended ceilings*

CP 290	: Suspended ceilings	Type and size of tile, boards, panels or strips
		Method of fixing
		Spacing of supports
		Perimeter detail
		Access panels

L   WINDOWS/DOORS/STAIRS

L1 Windows/Rooflights/Screens/ Louvres	L10 Timber windows/rooflights/ screens/louvres* L11 Metal windows/rooflights/ screens/louvres* L12 Plastics windows/rooflights/ screens/louvres
L2 Doors/Shutters/Hatches	L20 Timber doors/shutters/hatches* L21 Metal doors/shutters/hatches* L22 Plastics/Rubber doors/shutters/ hatches
L3 Stairs/Galleries/Balustrades	L30 Timber stairs/walkways/ balustrades* L31 Metal stairs/walkways/ balustrades*
L4 Glazing	L40 General glazing* L41 Lead light glazing L42 Infill panels/sheets

BS 8000   : Workmanship on building sites
  (Part 5)   : Carpentry, joinery, general fixings – L10, L20, L30
  (Part 7)   : Glazing – L40, L41, L42

L1   Windows/Rooflights/Screens/Louvres

L10 Timber windows/rooflights/screens/louvres

BS 1186   : Workmanship in
                 joinery

Casement windows/borrowed lights
  BS 644   : Windows
    1186
    (Part 3)   : Wood trim
    1227   : Hinges

  CP 153
    (Part 1)   : Cleaning and safety
    (Part 2)   : Durability and
                 maintenance
    (Part 3)   : Sound insulation

Generally – material
Casements:
  thickness
  division into panes and size of bars
  glazing beads
  treatment of bottom rails and
    meeting stiles if not detailed
  hinges etc. (where supplied with the
    component)
Frames:
  section: jambs and head
  ditto: sill (state if different material)

ditto: transome (ditto)
beads to swing casements
Jamb linings
Architraves and cover fillets

Double-hung sash windows		Generally – material
BS 644	: Windows	Sashes:
1186	: Wood trim	thickness
(Part 3)		division into panes and size of bars
		horns
		glazing beads
CP 153		treatment of bottom and meeting
(Part 1)	: Cleaning and safety	rails if not detailed
(Part 2)	: Durability and	
	maintenance	
(Part 3)	: Sound insulation	

Boxed frames
inside and outside linings
pulley stiles and pocket pieces
back linings
parting slip
parting bead
inside bead
sill
Boxed mullions (as for frames)
Jamb linings
Architraves and cover fillets

Frames for metal windows	All as frames to casement windows
BS 1285	

L11 *Metal windows/rooflights/screens/louvres*

Metal windows		As for timber windows (L10) except BS
BS 5286	: Aluminium framed	windows which can be specified by
	sliding glass	their reference number
	doors	Make clear whether fixing is by
6510	: Steel windows, sills,	contractor or specialist
	window boards	If by specialist, contractor probably
	and doors	must distribute to positions, cut and
CP 153		pin lugs and bed frames
(Part 1)	: Cleaning and safety	If in wood frames reference to them
(Part 2)	: Durability and	
	maintenance	
(Part 3)	: Sound insulation	

L2   Doors/Shutters/Hatches

L20 Timber doors/shutters/hatches

BS 1186	: Workmanship in joinery
CP 151 (Part 1)	: Timber doors

Ledged (and braced) doors

BS 459	: Matchboarded doors
1227	: Hinges

Generally – material
Each type of door:
  thickness of boarding
  width of boards and type of joint
  thickness of ledges
  fixings and fastenings (where supplied
    with the component)

Framed, ledged and braced doors

As for ledged and braced, but giving
  thickness of stiles and rails instead of
  ledges and stating whether boarding
  is filled in or sheathed (over middle
  and bottom rails)

Panelled doors, etc.

BS 1227	: Hinges

Generally – material
Each type of door
  thickness of stiles and rails
  number of panels
  thickness of panels
  design of panel on each face,
  e.g. square framed, moulded, etc.
  if part glazed, number of panes and
  size of bars
  glazing (where supplied with the
  component)
  fixings and fastenings (where
  supplied with the components)

Flush doors

BS 1227	: Hinges
4787	: Door sets, door leaves and frames

Whether for internal or external use
Thickness
Ply facing – if for staining to be stated
Core
Glue
Fixings and fastenings (where supplied
  with the component)

Door linings or frames and architraves

BS 1186 (Part 3)	: Wood trim
1567	: Wood door frames and linings

Material
Jamb linings: thickness
Wood frames:
  section: jambs and head
  ditto: transome

ditto: threshold (state if different
material)
Architraves and cover fillets

L21 Metal doors/shutters/hatches

Metal doors   Generally – material
  BS 5286   : Aluminium sliding   Size and thickness
                  doors   Frame
                        Fittings

Metal door frames   Profile of frame
  BS 1245   Size of opening
                        Method of fixing

L3   Stairs/Galleries/Balustrades

L30 Timber stairs/walkways/balustrades

Stairs
  BS 585   : Wood stairs   Treads, landings and risers: thickness of
       1186   : Workmanship in   each
               joinery   Construction
                        Wall strings: thickness and finish to top
                           edge
                        Outer strings: ditto, also whether cut or
                           close, finish to bottom edge and
                           framing to newels
                        Applied mouldings to strings
                        Skirtings to landings
                        Newels: size, design and finish to top
                        Balusters: size, design, spacing and
                         framing of ends
                        Solid balustrades: as for panelled
                         framings
                        Hand-rail: material, section and framing
                        Spandril framing: as for cupboard
                         fronts
                        Soffite of stairs, if matchboarded, ply
                         covered, etc.

L31 Metal stairs/walkways/balustrades

Staircases

Metal staircases, e.g. external escape stairs or steps and landings in machine rooms, etc., will usually be erected by specialists and be the subject of a PC sum

Tubular rails, balustrades, etc.

BS 1387	: Steel tubes and tubulars	
1740	: Wrought steel pipe fittings	
4127	: Stainless steel tubes	
4360	Weldable structural steels	
4604	Use of high strength friction grip bolts	

Wrought iron or steel
Size of members
Fittings – e.g. bends, tees, crosses, etc.
Jointing – e.g. screwed or welded
Finish – e.g. black or galvanised

L4   Glazing

L40 General glazing

Materials and workmanship

BS 544	: Linseed oil putty
952	: Glass for glazing
6262	: Code of practice for glazing

Sheet glass
General obscure glass
Any other kinds of glass to be used
Putty for glazing to wood
Ditto for glazing to metal
Sprigged and front and back puttied
Where to be glazed with beads
    (reference to beads in L10 timber windows or as supplied with metal windows L11)
Extent of bedding in washleather or velvet

General glazing

Each kind of glass in turn with extent of its use
Polished edges, etching, etc.
Bending

M   SURFACE FINISHES

M1	Screeds/trowelled flooring	M10	Sand cement/Concrete/ Granolithic screeds/flooring*
		M11	Mastic asphalt flooring*
		M12	Trowelled bitumen/resin/rubber- latex flooring*
M2	Plastered coatings	M20	Plastered/Rendered/Roughcast coatings*
		M21	Insulation with rendered finish
		M22	Sprayed mineral fibre coatings
		M23	Resin bound mineral coatings
M3	Work related to plastered coatings	M30	Metal mesh lathing/Anchored reinforcement for plastered coatings*
		M31	Fibrous plaster*
M4	Rigid tiles	M40	Stone/Concrete/Quarry/ Ceramic tiling/Mosaic*
		M41	Terrazzo tiling/In situ terrazzo*
		M42	Wood block/Composition block/Parquet flooring*
M5	Flexible sheet/tile coverings	M50	Rubber/Plastics/Cork/Lino/ Carpet tiling/sheeting*
		M51	Edge fixed carpeting*
		M52	Decorative papers/fabrics*
M6	Painting	M60	Painting/Clear finishing*

BS 8000	:	Workmanship on building sites
(Part 9)	:	Cement/Sand floor screeds and concrete floor toppings – M10
(Part 10)	:	Plastering and rendering – M20, M30
(Part 11.1)	:	Wall and floor tiling; ceramic, terrazzo, mosaic – M40, M41
(Part 11.2)	:	natural stone – M40
(Part 12)	:	Decorative wall coverings and painting – M52, M60

M1   Screeds/trowelled flooring

M10   Sand cement/Concrete/Granolithic screeds/flooring

Screeds		Composition
BS 4551	: Testing screeds	Floor screeds with thicknesses
		Ditto to steps and landings, etc.

Wall screeds with ditto
Mat spaces
Angle fillets for turn-up of felt roofing
Filling to access covers

Granolithic
  BS 882   : Aggregates for   Mix and colouring (if any)
                    granolithic   Pavings with thicknesses
                    concrete floors   Ditto to steps and landings, etc.
                                         Carborundum finish
                                         Non-slip nosings
                                         Finish to skirtings, strings, kerbs, etc.
                                         Floor strips

M11 Mastic asphalt flooring

Paving   Floors: thickness and colour (if
  BS 6577   : (natural rock)   coloured)
     6925   : (limestone   Skirtings: thickness, height and finish to
                    aggregate)   top edge
                    (coloured)
  CP 204   : In situ floor
                    finishes

M12 Trowelled bitumen/resin/rubber-latex flooring

Jointless floors   Type, thickness and colour
  CP 204   : In situ floor   Skirtings and covers
                    finishes   Floor strips

M2   Plastered coatings

M20 Plastered/Rendered/Roughcast coatings

Materials and workmanship   Portland cement
  BS 12   : Cement   Coloured cements
     890   : Limes   Sand
     1191   : Gypsum building   Waterproofing compound
                    plasters   Lime
                 : Premixed light-   Plaster board
                    weight plasters   Hard plaster
     1199–1200 : Sands for   Any special plaster (e.g. barium or
                    plastering and   vermiculite)
                    external   Fibre reinforcement, hair, etc.
                    rendering   Mix of each coat of plaster

1230	: Gypsum plaster board	Interval between coats, scoring undercoats, finish to face, etc.
4049	: Glossary of terms	Cement and sand mixes
4551	: Testing plaster/render	Protection
5262	: Code of Practice for external rendered finishes	
5270	: Bonding agents	
5492	: Code of practice for internal plastering	

Generally	Temporary rules for plastering and for specialists work
Plastering to ceilings and beams	Type of plaster Number of coats Salient angles Describe any system for suspension, or provisional sum if by specialist
Coves and cornices	Cove or cornice between ceiling and wall finish Ditto between ceiling and beam finish Bracketing
Wall plastering	Type of plaster Number of coats Dado plastering (if different) Coves Salient angles Dado mouldings, etc.
Skirtings	Material Number of coats Joints with wall and floor finishes
Cement work	Plain face, etc., to walls ⎫ As for wall Roughcast, stucco, etc. ⎭ plastering Cornices, pilasters, quoins and other features

M3   Work related to plastered coatings

M30 Metal mesh lathing/Anchored reinforcement for plastered coatings

| Metal lathing
  BS 1369 | Gauge and mesh
Method of fixing
Ceilings and beams
Pipe casings or other surfaces |

M31 Fibrous plaster

Fibrous plaster   Method of fixing
                                         Grounds (references to G20)
                                         Girths of cornices, etc.
                                         Where work is more elaborate, a
                                             general description with reference to
                                             detail drawings

M4   Rigid tiles

M40 Stone/Concrete/Quarry/Ceramic tiling/Mosaic

Quarry tiles, etc.   Type and quality of tiles
   BS 1197   : Concrete flooring   Thickness, colour and size of tiles
                    tiles   Bedding and jointing material
   5385   : Code of practice   Floors
                    for natural stone   Steps, etc.
                    and composition   Skirtings
                    block flooring   Window sills, cappings, offsets, etc.
   6431   : Ceramic tiles   Coves and rounded edges
   CP 202   : Floor tiling

Glazed tiles   All as for quarry tiles (ordinary glazed
   BS 5385   : Code of practice   surface will be assumed unless
                    for wall and   'eggshell glaze' is specified)
                    floor tiling
   5980   : Adhesives
   6431   : Ceramic tiling

M41 Terrazzo tiling/In situ terrazzo

Terrazzo   PC sum for specialist's work, including
   BS 4131   : Terrazzo tiles   dividing strips
   4357   : Terrazzo units   State if screed by specialist
   5385   : Code of practice   Protection
                    for terrazzo tile
                    and slab
                    flooring
   CP 204   : In situ floor finishes

M42 Wood block/Composition block/Parquet flooring

Block floors   Materials   ⎫
   BS 1187   : Wood blocks for   Thickness   ⎪
                    floor   Pattern and border   ⎬   or
                                         Laying and cleaning off   ⎪ PC sum
                                         Polishing   ⎪
                                         Protection   ⎭

| Parquet floors | | As for block floors with reference to the |
| BS 4050 | : Mosaic parquet panels | item specifying the sub-floor |

M5 Flexible sheet/tile coverings

M50 Rubber/Plastics/Cork/Lino/Carpet tiling/sheeting

Tile floors		Thickness and size of tiles
BS 1711	: Rubber	Make and colour
2592	: Thermoplastic flooring tiles	Laying
		Protection
3260	: Semi-flexible PVC floor tiles	
5325	: Installation of textile floor coverings	
5442	: Adhesives	
6826	: Linoleum and cork carpet tiles	
8203	: Code of practice for installation of tile flooring	
Sheet floors		Thickness
BS 1711	: Rubber	Make and colour
3261	: Flexible PVC flooring	Laying
		Protection
5442	: Adhesives	
6826	: Linoleum and cork carpet sheet	
8203	: Code of practice for installation of sheet flooring	

M51 Edge fixed carpeting

BS 5325	: Installation	Type of manufacturer's reference or PC sum
		Underlay
		Method of fixing
		Jointing/cover strips
		Stair nosings

M52 Decorative papers/fabrics

Paperhanging		Lining paper
BS 3046	: Adhesives for hanging flexible wall coverings	Decorative paper/fabric or PC price per piece
		Borders, etc.
3357	: Glue, size	

M6 Painting

M60 Painting/Clear finishing

Materials and workmanship

BS 381C	: Colours for identification coding and special purposes
1070	: Black paint (tar base)
1282	: Guide to the choice, use and application of wood preservatives
1336	: Knotting
1710	: Colour identification of pipelines and services
2015	: Glossary of paint terms
2523	: Lead based priming paints
3698	: Calcium plumbate priming paints
3900	: Methods of tests for paints
3981	: Iron oxide pigments
4764	: Powder cement paints
4800	: Paint colours for building purposes
5082	: Water-borne priming paints for woodwork
5358	: Solvent-borne priming paints for woodwork
5707	: Solutions of wood preservatives in organic solvents
6044	: Pavement marking paints

Ceiling emulsion
Wall emulsion
Cement paint
Flat wall paint (or other material for treatment of ceilings and walls)
Bituminous paint
Priming, undercoats and finishing paint for wood and metal work
Wood stain
Polish
Delivery and dilution of paint
Tints and selection
Surfaces dry – rubbing down coats – interval between coats – stippling, etc.
Any prohibition of spraying

6150	: Code of Practice Painting of buildings
6952	: Exterior wood coating

Finishes

If finishes are more or less uniform throughout they can be specified in turn under the following heads:
Ceilings
Walls
Dadoes
External cement work
Internal metalwork
External metalwork
Internal woodwork
External woodwork

If the specification becomes at all complicated it is more satisfactory to set it out in the form of a schedule with explanatory notes to simplify the references, e.g.:

ROOM	CEILING	WALLS	DADO	METALWORK	WOODWORK	REMARKS
1	Emul.	Emul.	–	Gloss	Gloss	
2	Emul.	Flat	Gloss	Gloss	Gloss	Dado 1.00 m high
etc., etc.,						

Notes: Emul. = twice emulsion
Flat   = prime and paint two coats flat wall paint
Gloss = prime and paint two undercoats and one coat hard gloss finish
All dadoes to be finished with 10 mm painted line cut in on both edges
    Heights are from top of skirting
Etc., etc.

Where walls of a room are to be in different colours, this should be made clear, just as painting of woodwork should be stated to be 'in multi-colours' when panels, etc., are to be picked out

N   FURNITURE/EQUIPMENT

N1   General purpose fixtures/
     furnishings/equipment

N10   General fixtures/furnishings/
      equipment*
N11   Domestic kitchen fittings*
N12   Catering equipment
N13   Sanitary appliances/fittings*
N14   Interior landscape
N15   Signs/Notices*

N2   Special purpose fixtures/
     furnishings/equipment

N20 ⎫
N21 ⎪   Appropriate section titles
N22 ⎬   for each project
N23 ⎭

N1   General purpose fixtures/furnishings/equipment

N10 General fixtures/furnishings/equipment
N11 Domestic kitchen fittings

Shelving

Thickness, widths and number of tiers
   in each position
Open slatted shelving: size and spacing
   of battens and ledges
Wall bearers
Posts, legs, rails, etc.
Brackets

Cupboards
  BS 1195   : Kitchen fitments
     3444   : Blockboard and
                laminboard
     5669   : Chipboard
     6222   : Domestic kitchen
                equipment

Cupboard fronts or doors and frames
Tops, bottoms, ends and divisions
Locks or other fastenings
Shelving or other fitting up
Bearers or brackets in the case of wall
   cupboards

Sundry joinery

The sizes of the various members and
   their method of assembly
Pelmets
Cloak rails
Backboards
Seats
Dressers
Counters
Racks or special fitments

Sundry glass items	Thickness: size: finish
	Mirrors
	Shelves
	Window sills, etc.
	Splashbacks

Sundry items
  BS 792   : Dustbins

Sundry items e.g. Curtain tracks, door mats, lockers, dustbins, etc., will usually be specified by maker's or merchant's catalogue number or be the subject of PC prices

N13 Sanitary appliances/fittings

Sanitary fittings
  BS 1125   : Flushing cisterns
                       for w.c's
  1188   : Ceramic
                       washbasins
  1189   : Cast iron baths
  1206   : Fireclay sinks
  1212   : Float operated
                       valves
  1244   : Metal sinks
  1254   : W.c. seats (plastic)
  1329   : Metal lavatory
                       basins
  1390   : Sheet steel baths
  1415   : Mixing valves
  1876   : Urinal cisterns
  1968   : Floats for ball
                       valves (copper)
  2081   : Chemical closets
  2456   : Floats for ball
                       valves (plastic)
  4305   : Baths made of
                       acrylic sheet
  5388   : Spray taps
  5503–6   : W.c. pans, bidets,
                       wash basins
  5779   : Spray mixing taps
  6340   : Shower units
  6465   : Code of practice
  6731   : Handrinse basins
  7015   : Cast acrylic sheets
                       for baths and
                       shower trays

Manufacturer's reference and fixing or PC sum with clear and sufficient description of each type of fitting to enable fixing to be priced (e.g. whether brackets are screwed or cantilever type, whether the sum includes flush pipes or not)

Towel rails

Toilet roll holders

N15 *Signs/Notices*

Signwriting		Description of work, style and size of
BS 5499	: Fire safety signs, etc.	letters, etc., so far as not shown on drawings
		Notices: size, material, lettering, fixing

P BUILDING FABRIC SUNDRIES

P1 Sundry proofing/insulation	P10 Sundry insulation/proofing work/fire stops*
	P11 Foamed/Fibre/Bead cavity wall insulation
P2 Sundry finishes/fittings	P20 Unframed isolated trims/skirtings/sundry items*
	P21 Ironmongery*
	P22 Sealant joints
P3 Sundry work in connection with engineering services	P30 Trenches/Pipeways/Pits for buried engineering services*
	P31 Holes/Chases/Covers/Supports for services*

P1 Sundry proofing/insulation

P10 Sundry insulation/proofing work/fire stops

Insulating quilts, boards, etc.		Material thickness and method of fixing
BS 3837	: Polystyrene board	Over ceiling joists in roof space
4841	: Rigid foam board	In wooden upper floors
5803	: Roof insulation	In partitions
7021	: Code of practice for thermal insulation of roofs externally	To tanks, cisterns, etc.

P2 Sundry finishes/fittings

P20 Unframed isolated trims/skirtings/sundry items

Skirtings		Material
BS 1186	: Wood trim	Thickness and height
(Part 3)		Description of section, e.g. moulded, etc.
		Backings
		Floor fillets
Cornices, frieze rails and dado rails		Material
BS 1186	: Wood trim	Dimensions
(Part 3)		Description of section
		Grounds

Angle brackets for cornices
Bracketing for plaster cornices,
pilasters, etc.

P21 *Ironmongery*

BS 3827   : Glossary of terms
                  for builders'
                  hardware

Door and window ironmongery   Hinges, latch or lock and other
BS 1227   : Hinges   furniture to doors, e.g. bolts, push
    2911   : Letter plates   plates, kicking plates, cabin hooks,
    4951 ⎱   etc.
    5872 ⎰   : Locks, latches   Hinges or pivots, fasteners and stays to
    5725   : Emergency exit   casement windows
                  devices   Sash lines or chains, pulleys, weights,
    6125   : Sash lines   fasteners, lifts and pulls to sash
    6459   : Door closers   windows

Sundry ironmongery, etc.   Water bars: material and section
BS 1161   : Aluminium alloy   Floor strips: ditto
                  sections   Dowels: ditto
    1494   : Fixing accessories Hand-rail brackets
                                     Shelf brackets

P3   Sundry work in connection with engineering services

P30 *Trenches/Pipeways/Pits for buried engineering services*

BS 5834   : Valve boxes   Trenches for water, electric or gas mains
                                         Excavation
                                         Beds
                                         Haunching
                                         Surrounds
                                     Meter pits, stop valve pits, etc.
                                     Stop valve boxes, access/inspection
                                         chambers including covers

P31 *Holes/Chases/Covers/Supports for services*

Forming/Cutting holes, mortices,   Size, material, making good
    chases, etc.
Trench covers   Material and design
                                     Material and sections of kerbs or
                                         bearers

Q   PAVING/PLANTING/FENCING/SITE FURNITURE

Much of the specification for work in this section for groundworks to roads, pavings, etc. will be covered in other sections, leaving such matters as asphalt road covering, planting, turfing, seeding, fencing, site furniture, etc. to be covered in this section.

Q1   Edgings for pavings

Q2   Pavings

Q3   Site planting

Q4   Fencing

Q5   Site furniture

Q10   Stone/Concrete/Brick kerbs/ edgings/channels*

Q20   Hardcore/Granular/Cement bound bases/sub-bases to roads/pavings*

Q21   In situ concrete roads/pavings/ bases

Q22   Coated macadam/Asphalt roads/pavings*

Q23   Gravel/Hoggin roads/pavings

Q24   Interlocking brick/block roads/ pavings

Q25   Slab/Brick/Sett/Cobble pavings*

Q26   Special surfacings/pavings for sport

Q30   Seeding/Turfing*
Q31   Planting*

Q40   Fencing*

Q50   Site/Street furniture/equipment*

Q1   Edgings for pavings

Q10   Stone/Concrete/Brick kerbs/edgings/channels

BS 435	: Dressed natural stone Kerbs, channels, etc.	Excavation or making up levels Foundation Kerbs/Edgings/Channels
7263	: Flags, kerbs, channels, edgings and quadrants	

Q2   Pavings

Q20 Hardcore/Granular/Cement bound bases/sub-bases to roads/pavings

Sub-base

Levelling and compacting sub-grade
Sub-base material to be used
Maximum thickness of layers and
   method of consolidation
Extent of thickness (after consolidation)
Blinding top surface
Any finishing to falls

Q22 Coated macadam/Asphalt roads/pavings

BS 594	: Rolled asphalt	Number of layers and finished thickness
1446 }	Mastic asphalt for	of each
1447 }	: roads and	Type of aggregate and grading of each
	footways	layer
3690	: Bitumens	Falls, cambers and rolling
4987	: Coated macadam	Gritting or other surface finish
	for roads and	
	pavings	
5273	: Dense tar road	
	surfacing	

Q25 Slab/Brick/Sett/Cobble pavings

BS 6677	: Clay and calcium-	Type size and thickness of material
	silicate paviers	Bedding
7263	: Flags, kerbs,	Laying to falls
	edgings and	Pattern
	quadrants	Steps

Q3   Site planting

BS 4428	: Recommendations
	for general
	landscaping
	operations

Q30 Seeding/Turfing

Lawns and banks	Excavation or making up levels
	Trimming banks
	Soiling (giving thickness)
	Grass seed (quality and weight per metre)
	Turf

Q31 Planting

Flower beds	Moving of reserved vegetable soil, depositing, levelling, breaking up and raking over
Trees, shrubs and other planting	Usually a provisional sum for work by specialists
	As this work is normally carried out after the main building work is finished, it is often excluded from the building contract and dealt with direct by the Employer

Q4   Fencing

Q40 Fencing

Fencing

		Type of fencing and spacing of posts with their stays
BS 1485	: Galvanised wire netting	Foundation to posts and stays
1722	: Fencing	In-filling between posts with method of fixing
4092		
(Part 1)	: Metal gates	Gates, posts, hinges and furniture (where part of fencing)
(Part 2)	: Wooden gates	
4102	: Steel wire	

Q5   Site furniture

Q50 Site/Street furniture/equipment

		Gate posts, hinges and furniture (where not part of fencing)
BS 4092		
(Part 1)	: Metal gates	
(Part 2)	: Wooden gates	
5649	: Lighting columns	
5696	: Play equipment	

R DISPOSAL SYSTEMS

R1 Drainage

R10 Rainwater pipework/gutters*
R11 Foul drainage above ground*
R12 Drainage below ground*
R13 Land drainage
R14 Laboratory/Industrial waste
　　　 drainage

R2 Sewerage

R20 Sewage pumping*
R21 Sewage treatment/sterilisation

R3 Refuse disposal

R30 Centralised vacuum cleaning
R31 Refuse chutes*
R32 Compactors/Macerators
R33 Incineration plant

BS 8000　　　: Workmanship on building sites
　(Part 13)　: Above ground drainage and sanitary appliances – R10, R11
　(Part 14)　: Below ground drainage – R12

R1 Drainage

R10 Rainwater pipework/gutters

Cast iron rainwater pipes
　BS 460　　　　: Cast iron rainwater
　　　　　　　　 goods

Quality, section (round or rectangular)
　and size of pipe
Any surface finish, e.g. galvanised
Method of jointing and fixing (e.g. ears
　or holderbats)
Bends, branches, etc.
Shoes or connection to drain
Outlet pieces from flat roofs
Connection pieces through roofs
Hopper heads and gratings

Cast iron eaves gutters
　BS 460　　　　: Cast iron rainwater
　　　　　　　　 goods

Quality, section and size
Any surface finish, e.g. galvanised
Method of jointing and fixing (e.g.
　brackets)
Angles, stop ends, etc.
Outlets and gratings

Pressed steel, asbestos-cement,
　aluminium, zinc or plastic rainwater
　goods

As for cast iron

BS 569	:	Asbestos-cement rainwater goods
1091	:	Pressed steel rainwater goods
1431	:	Wrought copper and wrought zinc rainwater goods
2997	:	Aluminium rainwater goods
4576	:	UPVC rainwater goods

Sheet steel gutters   Thickness of metal and method of
                                                          fixing
                                                     Any surface finish, e.g. galvanised
                                                     Angles, stop ends, outlets, etc.

Lead outlet or rainwater pipes   Outlet pipes from flats or gutters:
                                                          diameter, weight per metre,
                                                          connection to flat and connection (if
                                                          any) to other end
                                                     Weep pipes, etc.
                                                     Gratings

Lead rainwater heads   PC price and describe method of fixing
                                                     Gratings

R11 Foul drainage above ground

Wastes to basins, baths, sinks, etc.   Traps
   BS 1184   : Copper traps   Material and size of branch and main
      3380   : Wastes and   waste pipes in each case
                     overflows   Joint to fitting ⎫
      5255   : Plastic waste pipes   Joint of branch ⎬ With any brass
                     and fittings   to main pipe ⎭ ferrules, etc.
                                                     Joint of main pipe to gulley or drain
                                                     Grating to top of main pipe
                                                     Hopper head, where open wastes, and
                                                          grating

Ventilating pipes to wastes   Material and size
                                                     Point of and method of connection to
                                                          branch wastes and to main stack (or
                                                          if separate anti-syphon pipes)

Soil and ventilating pipes
BS 416	: Cast iron pipes	
3868	: Prefabricated galvanised steel stack units	
5572	: Sanitary pipework	

Material and size of branch and main soil pipes
Joint to fitting ⎱
Joint of branch ⎰ With any brass
to main pipe ⎭ ferrules,
thimbles, etc.
Joint of main pipe to drain
Grating to top of main pipe
Vent pipes to top of drains

Overflow pipes
BS 3380   : Wastes and overflows

Size and material
Method of jointing
Hinged flap or splay cut ends, etc.

Anti-siphon pipes

Material and size
Connection to soil pipe or arm of pan with ferrule
Point and method of connection to main stack

Testing

Requirements for testing

R12 *Drainage below ground*

Materials and workmanship
BS 65	: Clay drain and sewer pipes
437	: Cast iron socketed drain pipes
534	: Steel drain pipes
1194	: Concrete porous pipes
1196	: Clayware field drain pipes
1211	: Spun iron pipes
3656	: Asbestos-cement pipes
4660	: Unplasticised PVC
4772	: Ductile iron pipes
5911	: Precast concrete pipes and fittings for drainage and sewerage
6087	: Flexible joints for cast iron
8301	: Code of practice for building drainage

Cement
Sand
Mortar
Clayware or concrete field pipes
Salt-glazed ware pipes
Concrete pipes
Cast iron pipes
Pitch-fibre pipes
Drain excavation and backfilling
Concrete beds:
  width
  thickness
  haunching or surrounding
Laying and jointing of pipes

Runs of drains		Excavating and backfilling
		Any distinction in pipes to be used, e.g.
		  soil, surface water, inside building,
		  etc.
		Extent of concrete beds (if not to all)
		Minimum cover and extent of entirely
		  surrounding with concrete
		Any backfilling required in concrete
		Suspended drains (hangers, etc.)
		Bends, junctions, etc.
		Any special items, such as cleaning eyes
		Subsoil drainage

Gullies, etc.
  BS 65
     437
	
	: Clay ware
	: Cast iron
		Types of rainwater shoes and gullies
		  and their respective positions and
		  uses
		Gully kerbs

Manholes
  BS 497
 	
    1247
    7158
	
	: Cast iron and cast
	  steel covers and
	  frames
	: Step irons
	: Plastic inspection
	  chambers for
	  drains
		Sizes (if not indicated on drawings or in
		  a schedule)
		Excavation
		Concrete bottoms:
		  mix
		  thickness
		  spread beyond walls
		Walls:
		  bricks
		  mortar
		  thickness
		  internal finish
		Covers:
		  concrete slabs
		  iron covers, identified as to type and
		    weight
		  margins to covers
		Pipes:
		  main channels
		  branch channels
		  iron bolted inspection pipes with
		    branches
		  concrete benching and finish
		  intercepting trap
		Step irons:
		  minimum depth of manhole
		  spacing

Fresh air inlet		F.A.I. fitting Any length of vertical pipe and its fixing Pipe connection from manhole

Petrol interceptors	As for manholes including ventilation
Soakaways	Size and depth Bottom and walls (if any) Nature and extent of filling
Testing	Requirements for testing, e.g. water, smoke, etc. Make good defects

Note: In works of alteration the contractor cannot be expected to estimate the cost of making good defects to existing drains. Insert a provisional sum for this

R2 Sewerage

R20 Sewage pumping

Sewage disposal plant
 BS 6297 : Code of practice for design and installation of small sewage treatment works and cesspools
 8005   : Sewerage

Construction of tanks, filter beds, etc., on the same lines as manholes
Filtering media
Special ironwork: PC sum or makers' catalogue references
Pump (if any) and piping
Disposal of effluent

R3 Refuse disposal

R31 Refuse chutes

 BS 1703

Type and size of pipe
Method of fixing
Intake access
Outlet access

S PIPED SUPPLY SYSTEMS

S1	Water supply	S10	Cold water	
		S11	Hot water	
		S12	Hot and cold water (small scale)*	
		S13	Pressurised water	
		S14	Irrigation	
		S15	Fountains/Water features	
S2	Treated water supply	S20	Treated/Deionised/Distilled water	
		S21	Swimming pool water treatment	
S3	Gas supply	S30	Compressed air	
		S31	Instrument air	
		S32	Natural gas*	
		S33	Liquid petroleum gas	
		S34	Medical/Laboratory gas	
S4	Petrol/Oil storage	S40	Petrol/Oil – lubrication	
		S41	Fuel oil storage/distribution	
S5	Other supply systems	S50	Vacuum	
		S51	Steam	
S6	Fire fighting – water	S60	Fire hose reels	
		S61	Dry risers	
		S62	Wet risers	
		S63	Sprinklers	
		S64	Deluge	
		S65	Fire hydrants	
S7	Fire fighting – gas/foam	S70	Gas fire fighting	
		S71	Foam fire fighting	

BS 8000   : Workmanship on building sites
(Part 15) : Hot and cold water services (domestic) – S12

As an example of specification information required, Sections S12 and S32, representing as they do supplies for a domestic building, are chosen. The remaining sections are of a special nature and would in all probability be matters dealt with by a specialist engineer.

S1 Water supply

S12 Hot and cold water (small scale)

Materials and workmanship
   BS 486   : Asbestos-cement
                  pressure pipes

Steel tubing:
   quality and if galvanised
   jointing and fixing

BS 534	: Steel spigot and socket pipes	bends, tees, etc.

Copper tubing:
  quality and gauges
  jointing and fixing
  type of couplings, etc.

1010	: Draw-off valves and stop valves
1211	: Spun iron pipes
1387	: Steel tubes
1740	: Wrought steel pipe fittings
2871	: Copper and copper alloy tubes
2879	: Draining taps
3284	: Polyethylene pipe for cold water services
3380	: Wastes
3457	: Materials for tap washers
3505	: UPVC pipes for cold potable water supply
3974	: Pipe supports
4118	: Glossary of terms
4346	: Joints and fittings for use with unplasticised PVC pipes
5292	: Jointing materials and compounds
5556	: Thermoplastic pipes
5572	: Sanitary pipe work
6700	: Water supply for domestic use
6730	: Polyethylene pipes

Polythene tubing:
  quality and gauges
  butt welding and bending
  compression fittings or other method
    of jointing
Joints of different materials

Connection to water main	Refer to A53 with a definition of extent of Authority's work
Service up to building	Material and size Stopcock Wrapping pipe Stopcock inside building
Rising main and branches	Material and size Connection to cistern and ball valve Branches to drinking water or other points requiring main service Branch to heating engineers' feed cistern Stopcocks controlling branches

Storage cistern   Material and size of cistern
    BS 417   : Galvanised steel   Ditto of overflow pipe
                     cisterns   Coupling up (if more than one)
     1563   : Cast iron sectional
                     tanks
     1564   : Pressed steel ditto
     4213   : Cold water storage
                     cisterns

Down services   Material and size at outlet of cistern
                                                    Stopcock near cistern
                                                    Sizes and general arrangement of
                                                       distribution pipes or reference to lay-
                                                       out shown on drawings
                                                    Stopcocks controlling branches
                                                    Provision for draining any dips below
                                                       draw-off level
                                                    Service to hot water system: material
                                                       and size and controlling stopcock

Hot water service   Sizes and general arrangement of
    BS 699   : Copper cylinders   distribution pipes etc., as for down
     1565   : Galvanised steel   services
                     indirect   Cylinder
                     cylinders   Controls
     1566   : Copper ditto   Heated towel rails
     3198   : Copper storage
                     units
     5422   : Specification for
                     insulation
                     materials

Chlorinating   Chlorinating water pipes

Testing   Requirements for testing plumbing
                                                       work

S3 Gas supply

S32 Natural gas

Service up to meter   Refer to A53 with a definition of extent
                                                       of Authority's work

Distribution pipes   Material and size of pipes, general
                                                       arrangement or reference to lay-out
                                                       on drawings
                                                    Gas cocks

Fittings			Any special connections to be supplied, e.g. brass tube, flexible connections, etc.
BS 669	:	Flexible metallic tubing	
746	:	Gas meter unions	
1552	:	Manual shut off valves	
6400	:	Installation of meters	

Testing   Requirements for testing pipework

T MECHANICAL HEATING/COOLING/REFRIGERATION SYSTEMS

T1	Heat source	T10	Gas/Oil fired boilers
		T11	Coal fired boilers
		T12	Electrode/Direct electric boilers
		T13	Packaged steam generators
		T14	Heat pumps
		T15	Solar collectors
		T16	Alternative fuel boilers
T2	Primary heat distribution	T20	Primary heat distribution
T3	Heat distribution/utilisation – water	T30	Medium temperature hot water heating
		T31	Low temperature hot water heating
		T32	Low temperature hot water heating (small scale)*
		T33	Steam heating
T4	Heat distribution/utilisation – air	T40	Warm air heating
		T41	Warm air heating (small scale)
		T42	Local heating units
T5	Heat recovery	T50	Heat recovery
T6	Central refrigeration/ Distribution	T60	Central refrigeration plant
		T61	Primary/Secondary cooling distribution
T7	Local cooling/Refrigeration	T70	Local cooling units
		T71	Cold rooms
		T72	Ice pads

As an example of specification information required section T32 represents a domestic heating system. The remaining sections are of a special nature and would in all probability be matters dealt with by a specialist engineer.

T3   Heat distribution/utilisation – water

T32 Low temperature hot water heating (small scale)

BS 779	: Boilers for heating and hot water	Heat source
		Pipework and fixing

3377	: Back boilers (domestic)	Radiators, heaters, etc. Pumps, fittings, etc.
4433	: Solid smokeless fuel boilers	Insulation Testing
5449	: Code of Practice for central heating	
6880	: Code of practice for low temperature hot water heating systems	

Sections U–X are for specialist work generally outside the scope of this book and the entries that follow under these headings are restricted to the CAWS first and third levels to indicate the grouping of the detailed specification for these items which will be required.

U   VENTILATION/AIR CONDITIONING SYSTEMS

U1	Ventilation/Fume extract	U10	General supply/extract
		U11	Toilet extract
		U12	Kitchen extract
		U13	Car parking extract
		U14	Smoke extract/Smoke control
		U15	Safety cabinet/Fume cupboard extract
		U16	Fume extract
		U17	Anaesthetic gas extract
U2	Industrial extract	U20	Dust collection
U3	Air conditioning – all air	U30	Low velocity air conditioning
		U31	VAV air conditioning
		U32	Dual-duct air conditioning
		U33	Multi-zone air conditioning
U4	Air conditioning – air/water	U40	Induction air conditioning
		U41	Fan-coil air conditioning
		U42	Terminal re-heat air conditioning
		U43	Terminal heat pump air conditioning
U5	Air conditioning – hybrid	U50	Hybrid system air conditioning
U6	Air conditioning – local	U60	Free standing air conditioning units
		U61	Window/Wall air conditioning units
U7	Other air systems	U70	Air curtains

V ELECTRICAL SUPPLY/POWER/ LIGHTING SYSTEMS

V1 Generation/Supply/HV
    distribution

V10 Electricity generation plant
V11 HV supply/distribution/public
     utility supply
V12 LV supply/public utility supply

V2 General LV distribution/
    lighting/power

V20 LV distribution
V21 General lighting
V22 General LV power

V3 Special types of supply/
    distribution

V30 Extra low voltage supply
V31 DC supply
V32 Uninterrupted power supply

V4 Special lighting

V40 Emergency lighting
V41 Street/Area/Floor lighting
V42 Studio/Auditorium/Arena
     lighting

V5 Electric heating

V50 Electric underfloor heating
V51 Local electric heating units

V9 General/Other electrical work

V90 General lighting and power
     (small scale)

W   COMMUNICATIONS/SECURITY/ CONTROL SYSTEMS

W1	Communications – speech/audio	W10	Telecommunications
		W11	Staff paging/location
		W12	Public address/Sound amplification
		W13	Centralised dictation
W2	Communications – audio-visual	W20	Radio/TV/CCTV
		W21	Projection
		W22	Advertising display
		W23	Clocks
W3	Communications – data	W30	Data transmission
W4	Security	W40	Access control
		W41	Security detection and alarm
W5	Protection	W50	Fire detection and alarm
		W51	Earthing and bonding
		W52	Lightning protection
		W53	Electromagnetic screening
W6	Control	W60	Monitoring
		W61	Central control
		W62	Building automation

X   TRANSPORT SYSTEMS

X1	People/Goods	X10	Lifts
		X11	Escalators
		X12	Moving pavements
X2	Goods/Maintenance	X20	Hoists
		X21	Cranes
		X22	Travelling cradles
		X23	Goods distribution/Mechanised warehousing
X3	Documents	X30	Mechanical document conveying
		X31	Pneumatic document conveying
		X32	Automatic document filing and retrieval

Sections Y and Z are for general reference specification for services and building items. Cross reference in other sections to the general reference specification will avoid inconsistencies and unnecessary repetition of like items. The CAWS levels are given to indicate the nature of such general reference items.

Y   SERVICES REFERENCE SPECIFICATION

Y1	Pipelines and ancillaries	Y10	Pipelines
		Y11	Pipeline ancillaries
Y2	General pipeline equipment	Y20	Pumps
		Y21	Water tanks/cisterns
		Y22	Heat exchangers
		Y23	Storage cylinders/calorifiers
		Y24	Trace heating
		Y25	Cleaning and chemical treatment
Y3	Air ductlines and ancillaries	Y30	Air ductlines
		Y31	Air ductline ancillaries
Y4	General air ductline equipment	Y40	Air handling units
		Y41	Fans
		Y42	Air filtration
		Y43	Heating/Cooling coils
		Y44	Humidifiers
		Y45	Silencers/Acoustic treatment
		Y46	Grilles/Diffusers/Louvres
Y5	Other common mechanical items	Y50	Thermal insulation
		Y51	Testing and commissioning of mechanical services
		Y52	Vibration isolation mountings
		Y53	Control components – mechanical
		Y54	Identification – mechanical
		Y59	Sundry common mechanical items
Y6	Cables and wiring	Y60	Conduit and cable trunking
		Y61	HV/LV cables and wiring
		Y62	Busbar trunking
		Y63	Support components – cables

Y7	General electrical equipment	Y70	HV switchgear
		Y71	LV switchgear and distribution boards
		Y72	Contactors and starters
		Y73	Luminaires and lamps
		Y74	Accessories for electrical services
Y8	Other common electrical items	Y80	Earthing and bonding components
		Y81	Testing and commissioning of electrical services
		Y82	Identification – electrical
		Y89	Sundry common electrical items
Y9	Other common mechanical and/or electrical items	Y90	Fixing to building fabric
		Y91	Off-site painting/Anti-corrosion treatments
		Y92	Motor drives – electric

Z   BUILDING FABRIC REFERENCE SPECIFICATION

Z1	Fabricating	Z10	Purpose made joinery
		Z11	Purpose made metalwork
Z2	Fixing/Jointing	Z20	Fixings/Adhesives
		Z21	Mortars
		Z22	Sealants
Z3	Finishing	Z30	Off-site painting

Appendix Example specification

The example specification is for a small extension to a typical suburban semi-detached house, an extension rendered necessary by a growing family who preferred to extend the house they liked rather than move to a larger house in a strange district. This is a set of circumstances that often faces young architects and surveyors.

For simple work it is often considered adequate to restrict the specification to notes on a drawing and this example could be considered a borderline case. There are however possible complications in the work: digging next to an adjoining owner; problems of stitching a metric extension onto an imperial building etc., and it may well be in the employer's best interest that a full specification is written. Borderline or not however the principle is the same.

The specification has been drafted using the Minor Works Version of the National Building Specification as the base document. For such a small project it was considered appropriate to edit the NBS clauses.

In order to keep the drawing simple and to aid the contractor's comprehension of what is required, a Schedule of Work has been prepared as section B of the specification. The Schedule of Work descriptions have been kept short and to the point by referring to relevant clauses in the subsequent sections which specify the quality of materials and workmanship.

The original specification for this extension was a hand drafted version prepared in the traditional manner. Although the architect did not go on an extended holiday as suggested in Chapter 1, the extension was built with the minimum of variations and to the complete satisfaction of the client and, it is hoped, the architect and the builder!

SPECIFICATION OF WORKS

Required in

CONSTRUCTION OF ADDITIONAL ACCOMMODATION

at

110 WHYTELEAFE HILL
WHYTELEAFE, SURREY

for

CHRISTOPHER J WILLIS ESQ.

DAVID J JUNIPER Dip Arch, RIBA
Chartered Architect
High Wold Gate
Woldingham
Surrey

October 1990

CONTENTS

A	Preliminaries/General conditions	1
B	Schedule of work and price collection	10
D20	Excavating and filling	14
E10	In situ concrete	14
E20	Formations/Formwork for in situ concrete	15
E30	Reinforcement for in situ concrete	15
F10	Brick/Block walling	16
F30	Accessories/Sundry items for brick/block walling	17
G20	Carpentry/Timber framing/First fixing	17
H71	Lead sheet flashings	18
J41	Built-up felt roof coverings	19
K11	Rigid sheet sheathing/linings	20
K20	Timber board flooring	21
L10	External screens	21
L20	Doors	22
L30	Stairs	22
L40	Glazing	23
M20	Plastered coatings	23
M60	Painting	24
N13	Sanitary appliances/fittings	24
P10	Sundry insulation	25
P20	Unframed isolated trims/skirtings/sundry items	25
R10	Rainwater pipework/gutters	25
Z10	Purpose made joinery	26
Z20	Fixings	26
Z21	Mortars	27
Z22	Sealants	27

A **PRELIMINARIES/GENERAL CONDITIONS**   £

A10 **PROJECT PARTICULARS**

120 EMPLOYER:
C.J. Willis FRICS FCIArb
110 Whyteleafe Hill,
Whyteleafe, Surrey.
Telephone: 081 123456

140 ARCHITECT (hereinafter referred to as 'CA'):
D.J. Juniper RIBA
High Wold Gate,
Woldingham, Surrey.
Telephone: 081 654321

A11 **DRAWINGS**

110 THE TENDER DRAWING: CW1 – Plans and details.

120 THE CONTRACT DRAWING will be the same as the tender drawing.

A13 **DESCRIPTION OF THE WORK**

120 THE WORK: Remove existing lean to carport, construct new carport with bedroom over connected to existing house half landing level on internal staircase.

A20 **THE CONTRACT**

910 MINOR WORKS AGREEMENT 1980: The form of contract will be the JCT Agreement for Minor Building Works 1980 including Supplementary Memorandum revised March 1988 and with Amendments MW5:1988 and MW6: 1989.
Allow for the obligations, liabilities and services described therein against the headings set out below:

The Works comprise extension to existing house

Recitals 1-5
1st Recital: The reference to Contract Administrator will be deleted
                The reference to Schedules will be deleted
2nd Recital: The reference to Schedules will be deleted
5th Recital: The 5th Recital will be deleted.

Articles 1–4
Article 4: The reference to Royal Institute of British Architects will be deleted

THE CONDITIONS

1.0   Intentions of the parties

2.0   Commencement and completion

2.1   The Works may be commenced not later than 6 weeks after acceptance of the tender and shall be completed within 13 weeks thereafter.

2.3   Liquidated damages: £100.00 per week or part of a week

2.5   Defects Liability Period: 3 months

To collection £

1

A   Preliminaries/General conditions (continued)   £

3.0	Control of the Works	
3.6	The reference to schedules will be deleted	
4.0	Payment	
4.1	The references to schedules will be deleted	
4.2	Retention percentage: 5%	
4.3	Penultimate certificate percentage: 97.5%	
4.4	Period for supply of documentation: 3 months	
4.5	Percentage addition: Nil %	
5.0	Statutory obligations	
5.2	Value Added Tax: Clause B1.1 of the Supplementary Memorandum applies	
6.0	Injury, damage and insurance	
6.2	Insurance cover to be not less than: £500,000.00	
6.3B	Clause 6.3A will be deleted	
7.0	Determination	
8.0	Supplementary Memorandum	
9.0	Settlement of disputes – Arbitration	

A30   TENDERING

110   SCOPE: These conditions are supplementary to those stated in the invitation to tender and on the Form of Tender.

170   ACCEPTANCE OF TENDER: The Employer and his representatives:
–   Offer no guarantee that the lowest or any tender will be recommended for acceptance or accepted.
–   Will not be responsible for any cost incurred in the preparation of any tender.

180   SITE VISIT: Before tendering, ascertain the nature of the site, access thereto and all local conditions and restrictions likely to affect the execution of the Works.

191   PERIOD OF VALIDITY: Tenders must remain open for consideration (unless previously withdrawn) for not less than 13 weeks from the date fixed for the submission or lodgement of tenders. Information on the date for possession/commencement is given in section A20.

310   SPECIFICATION WITHOUT QUANTITIES: Where and to the extent that quantities are not included in the specification, tenders must include for all work shown or described in the tender documents as a whole or clearly apparent as being necessary for the complete and proper execution of the Works.

320   PRICING OF SPECIFICATION: Alterations and qualifications to the specification must not be made without the written consent of the CA. Tenders containing such alterations or qualifications may be rejected. Costs relating to items in the specification which are not priced will be deemed to have been included elsewhere in the tender.

331   THE PRICED SPECIFICATION must be submitted within one week of request.

To collection £

A   Preliminaries/General conditions (continued)   £

421   FLUCTUATIONS: The list of materials, goods, etc. required by item A2.1 of the
         Supplementary Memorandum to the form of contract is to be provided by the Contractor
         and must be submitted within one week of request.
         Fuels must not be included in the list.

A31   PROVISION, CONTENT AND USE OF DOCUMENTS

DEFINITIONS AND INTERPRETATIONS

120   CA means the person nominated in the Contract as Architect or Contract Administrator
         or his authorised representative.

130   IN WRITING: When required to notify, inform, instruct, agree, confirm, obtain approval
         or obtain instructions do so in writing.

140   APPROVAL (and words derived therefrom) means the approval in writing of the CA
         unless specified otherwise.

181   CROSS-REFERENCES TO THE SPECIFICATION:
  –   Where a numerical cross-reference to a specification section or clause is given on
         drawings or other pricing document the Contractor must verify its accuracy by checking
         the remainder of the annotation or item description against the terminology used in the
         referred to section or clause.
  –   Where a cross-reference for a particular type of work, feature, material or product is
         given, relevant clause(s) elsewhere in the referred to specification section dealing with
         general matters, ancillary products and workmanship also apply.
  –   Where a cross-reference is not given, the relevant section(s) and clause(s) of the
         specification will apply.
  –   The Contractor must, before proceeding, obtain clarification or instructions in relation to
         any discrepancy or ambiguity which he may discover.

225   REFERENCES TO BSI DOCUMENTS are to the versions and amendments listed in the
         British Standards Catalogue current at the date of tender.

240   MANUFACTURERS' REFERENCES are those current at the date of tender and mean
         the particular product as specified in the manufacturer's technical literature current at
         that time.

250   EQUIVALENT PRODUCTS: Where the specification, by use of the words 'or equivalent',
         permits substitution of a product of different manufacture to that specified and such
         substitution is desired, before ordering the product submit for approval documentary
         evidence that the alternative product is equivalent.

270   SIZES: Unless otherwise stated:
  –   Products are specified by their co-ordinating sizes.
  –   Cross section dimensions of timber shown on drawings are nominal sizes before any
         required planing.

290   SUPPLY AND FIX: Unless stated otherwise all items given in the schedule of work
         and/or on the drawings are to be supplied and fixed complete.

TERMS USED IN ALTERATION

311   REMOVE means disconnect, dismantle as necessary and remove the stated element,
         work or component and all associated accessories, fastenings, supports, linings and
         bedding materials, and dispose of unwanted materials. It does not include removing
         associated pipework, wiring, ductwork or other services.

321   KEEP FOR REUSE means:
  –   During removal prevent damage to the stated components or materials, and clean off
         bedding and jointing materials.
  –   Stack neatly, adequately protect and store until required by the Employer or for use in
         the Works as instructed.

                                                              To collection £

A	Preliminaries/General conditions (continued)	£

351   MAKE GOOD means carry out local remedial work to components, features and finishes which have been disturbed by other, previous work under this Contract and leave in a sound and neat condition. It does not include:
- Replacement of components or parts of components.
- Redecoration.

The meaning of the term shall not be limited by this definition where used in connection with the defects liability provisions of the Contract.

DOCUMENTS PROVIDED ON BEHALF OF EMPLOYER

430   ADDITIONAL COPIES OF SPECIFICATION: After execution of the Contract, two copies of the Specification will be issued to the Contractor in accordance with the Contract. Additional copies will be issued on request, if available, but will be charged to the Contractor.

440   DIMENSIONS: The accuracy of dimensions scaled from the drawings is not guaranteed. Obtain from the CA any dimensions required but not given in figures on the drawings nor calculable from figures on the drawings.

460   THE SPECIFICATION: All sections of the specification must be read in conjunction with Preliminaries/General conditions.

A32   MANAGEMENT OF THE WORKS

120   INSURANCES: Before starting work on site submit documentary evidence and/or policies and receipts for the insurances required by the Conditions of Contract.

130   INSURANCE CLAIMS: If any event occurs which may give rise to any claim or proceeding in respect of loss or damage to the Works or injury or damage to persons or property arising out of the Works, forthwith give notice in writing to the Employer, the CA and the Insurers. Indemnify the Employer against any loss which may be caused by failure to give such notice.

290   NOTICE OF COMPLETION: Give CA at least 2 weeks notice of the anticipated dates of practical completion of the whole or parts of the Works.

461   INTERIM VALUATIONS: At least 7 days before the established dates for interim valuations submit to the CA details of amounts due under the Contract together with all necessary supporting information.

A33   QUALITY STANDARDS/CONTROL

MATERIALS AND WORK GENERALLY

110   GOOD PRACTICE: Where and to the extent that materials, products and workmanship are not fully detailed or specified they are to be:
- Of a standard appropriate to the Works and suitable for the purposes stated in or reasonably to be inferred from the project documents, and
- In accordance with good building practice.

121   GENERAL QUALITY OF PRODUCTS:
- Products to be new unless otherwise specified.
- For products specified to a British Standard obtain certificates of compliance from manufacturers when requested.
- Ensure that the whole quantity of each product required is of consistent kind, size, quality and overall appearance.

To collection £

A   Preliminaries/General conditions (continued)   £

131   PROPRIETARY PRODUCTS:
–   Handle, store, prepare and use or fix each product in accordance with its manufacturer's current printed or written recommendations. Inform CA if these conflict with any other specified requirement. Submit copies when requested.
–   The tender will be deemed to be based on the products as marketed and recommendations on their use current at the date of tender.
–   Where British Board of Agrément products are used, comply with the limitations, recommendations and requirements of the relevant valid certificates.

150   PROTECTION OF PRODUCTS/MATERIALS:
–   Prevent over-stressing, distortion and any other type of physical damage.
–   Keep clean and free from contamination. Prevent staining, chipping, scratching or other disfigurement, particularly of products exposed to view in the finished work.
–   Keep dry and in a suitably low humidity atmosphere to prevent premature setting, moisture movement and similar defects. Where appropriate store off the ground and allow free air movement around and between stored components.
–   Prevent excessively high or low temperatures and rapid changes of temperature in the material.
–   Protect adequately from rain, damp, frost, sun and other elements as appropriate. Ensure that materials are at a suitable temperature and moisture content at time of use.
–   Ensure that covers are of ample size, in good weatherproof condition and well secured.
–   Keep different types and grades of materials separately and adequately identified.
–   So far as possible keep materials in their original wrappings, packings or containers, with unbroken seals, until immediately before they are used.
–   Wherever possible retain protective wrappings after fixing and until shortly before Practical Completion.
–   Ensure that protective measures are fully compatible with and not prejudicial to the products/materials.

160   SUITABILITY OF PREVIOUS WORK AND CONDITIONS: Before starting each section of work, ensure that:
–   Previous, related work is appropriately complete, in accordance with the project documents, to a suitable standard and in a suitable condition to receive the new work.
–   All necessary preparatory work has been carried out, including provision for services, damp proofing, priming and sealing.
–   The environmental conditions are suitable, particularly that the building is suitably weathertight when internal components, services and finishes are installed.

170   GENERAL QUALITY OF WORKMANSHIP:
–   Operatives must be appropriately skilled and experienced for the type and quality of work.
–   Take all necessary precautions to prevent damage to the work from frost, rain and other hazards .
–   Inspect components/materials carefully before fixing or using and reject any which are defective.
–   Fix or lay securely, accurately and in alignment.
–   Where not specified otherwise, select fixing and jointing methods and types, sizes and spacings of fastenings in compliance with section Z20. Fastenings to comply with relevant British Standards.
–   Provide suitable, tight packings at screwed and bolted fixing points to take up tolerances and prevent distortion. Do not overtighten fixings.
–   Adjust location and fixing of components so that joints which are to be finished with mortar or sealant or otherwise left open to view are even and regular.
–   Ensure that all moving parts operate properly and freely. Do not cut, grind or plane prefinished components to remedy binding or poor fit without approval.

180   BS 8000: BASIC WORKMANSHIP:
–   Where compliance with BS 8000 is specified, this is only to the extent that the recommendations therein define the quality of the finished work.
–   If there is any conflict or discrepancy between the recommendations of BS 8000 on the one hand and the project documents on the other, the latter will prevail.

To collection £

A   Preliminaries/General conditions (continued)   £

ACCURACY/SETTING OUT GENERALLY

321   SETTING OUT: Check the levels and dimensions of the site against those shown on the drawings, and record the results on a copy of the drawings. Notify CA in writing of any discrepancies and obtain instructions before proceeding.

322   SETTING OUT: Inform CA when overall setting out is complete and before commencing construction.

340   APPEARANCE AND FIT:
–   Arrange the setting out, erection, juxtaposition of components and application of finishes (working within the practical limits of the design and the specification) to ensure that there is satisfactory fit at junctions, that there are no practically or visually unacceptable changes in plane, line or level and that the finished work has a true and regular appearance.
–   Wherever satisfactory accuracy, fit and/or appearance of the work are likely to be critical or difficult to achieve obtain approval of proposals or of the appearance of the relevant aspects of the partially finished work as early as possible.

SUPERVISION/INSPECTION/DEFECTIVE WORK

550   DEFECTS IN EXISTING CONSTRUCTION to be reported to CA without delay. Obtain instructions before proceeding with work which may:
–   Cover up or otherwise hinder access to the defective construction, or
–   Be rendered abortive by the carrying out of remedial work.

571   PROPOSALS FOR RECTIFICATION OF DEFECTIVE WORK/MATERIALS:
–   As soon as possible after any part(s) of the work or any materials or goods are known or appear to be not in accordance with the Contract, submit proposals to CA for opening up, inspection, testing, making good or removal and re-execution.
–   Allow for the possibility that such proposals may be unacceptable to the CA, and that he may issue instructions requiring removal from the site.

WORK AT OR AFTER COMPLETION

610   GENERALLY:
–   Make good all damage consequent upon the work.
–   Remove all temporary markings, coverings and protective wrappings unless otherwise instructed.
–   Clean the works thoroughly inside and out, remove all splashes, deposits, efflorescence, rubbish and surplus materials consequent upon the execution of the work.
–   Cleaning materials and methods to be as recommended by manufacturers of products being cleaned, and to be such that there is no damage or disfigurement to other materials or construction.

620   PAINTED SURFACES: Touch up minor faults in newly painted/repainted work, carefully matching colour, and brushing out edges. Repaint badly marked areas back to suitable breaks or junctions.

630   MOVING PARTS: Adjust, ease and lubricate moving parts of new work as necessary to ensure easy and efficient operation, including doors, windows, drawers, ironmongery, appliances, valves and controls.

650   MAKING GOOD DEFECTS: Make arrangements with the Employer and give reasonable notice of the precise dates for access to the various parts of the Works for purposes of making good defects. Inform CA when remedial works to the various parts of the Works are completed.

To collection £

A   Preliminaries/General conditions (continued)   £

A34   SECURITY/SAFETY/PROTECTION

GENERALLY

110   SECURITY: Adequately safeguard the site, the Works, products, materials, plant, and
           any existing buildings affected by the Works from damage and theft. Take all reasonable
           precautions to prevent unauthorised access to the site, the Works and adjoining
           property.

120   STABILITY: Accept responsibility for the stability and structural integrity of the Works
           during the Contract, and support as necessary. Prevent overloading: details of design
           loads may be obtained from CA.

130   OCCUPIED PREMISES: The existing house will be occupied and used during the
           Contract. Carry out the Works without undue inconvenience and nuisance and without
           danger to occupants and users.

PROTECT AGAINST THE FOLLOWING:

221   NOISE:
  –   Do not use pneumatic drills and other noisy appliances without consent of the CA.
  –   Do not use or permit employees to use radios or other audio equipment in ways or at
           times which may cause nuisance.

230   POLLUTION: Take all reasonable precautions to prevent pollution of the site, the Works
           and the general environment.

240   NUISANCE: Take all necessary precautions to prevent nuisance from smoke, dust,
           rubbish and other causes.

260   FIRE: Take all necessary precautions to prevent personal injury, death, and damage to
           the Works or other property from fire.

261   FIRE: Smoking will not be permitted on the site .

265   BURNING ON SITE of materials arising from the work will not be permitted.

280   MOISTURE: Prevent the work from becoming wet or damp where this may cause
           damage. Dry out the Works thoroughly. Control the drying out and humidity of the Works
           and the application of heat to prevent:
  –   Blistering and failure of adhesion.
  –   Damage due to trapped moisture.
  –   Excessive movement.

290   RUBBISH: Remove rubbish and debris from time to time and keep the site and Works
           clean and tidy. Remove all rubbish, dirt and residues from voids and cavities in the
           construction before closing in.

PROTECT THE FOLLOWING:

310   WORK IN ALL SECTIONS: Adequately protect all types of work and all parts of the
           Works throughout the Contract.

320   EXISTING SERVICES:
  –   Before starting work check positions of existing services.
  –   Adequately protect, and prevent damage to all services. Do not interfere with their
           operation without consent of the service authorities or private owners.
  –   If any damage to services results from the execution of the Works, notify CA and
           appropriate service authority without delay. Make arrangements for the work to be made
           good without delay to the satisfaction of the service authority or private owner as
           appropriate.

To collection £

A   Preliminaries/General conditions (continued)   £

330   ROADS AND FOOTPATHS: Any damage to roads and footpaths consequent upon the Works must be made good to the satisfaction of the Local Authority or private owner. Adequately maintain approaches to the site and keep clear of mud and debris.

340   TREES/HEDGES/SHRUBS/LAWNS: Adequately protect and preserve. Replace to approval or treat as instructed any species or areas damaged or removed without approval.

350   EXISTING FEATURES: Prevent damage to existing buildings, fences, gates, walls, roads, paved areas and other site features which are to remain in position during the execution of the Works.

360   EXISTING WORK: Prevent damage to existing property undergoing alteration or extension and make good to match existing any defects so caused. Cut away and strip out the minimum necessary and with care to reduce the amount of making good to a minimum.

365   BUILDING INTERIORS: Protect building interiors exposed to the weather during the course of alteration work with temporary enclosures of sufficient size to permit execution of the work and which will remain weathertight even in severe weather.

380   ADJOINING PROPERTY: Access to/use of adjoining property has been agreed with adjacent owners as follows: 112 Whyteleafe Hill for erection of retaining wall.

381   ADJOINING PROPERTY: Take all reasonable precautions to prevent damage to adjoining property. Obtain permission as necessary from the owners if requiring to erect scaffolding on or otherwise use adjoining property, and pay all charges. Clear away and make good on completion or when directed. Bear the cost of repairing any damage arising from execution of the Works.

390   EXISTING STRUCTURES:
–   Provide and maintain during the execution of the Works all incidental shoring, strutting, needling and other supports as may be necessary to preserve the stability of existing structures on the site or adjoining, that may be endangered or affected by the Works.
–   Support existing structure as necessary during cutting of new openings or replacement of structural parts.
–   Do not remove supports until new work is strong enough to support the existing structure. Prevent overstressing of completed work when removing supports.

A35   **SPECIFIC LIMITATIONS ON METHOD/SEQUENCE/ TIMING**

110   SCOPE: The limitations described in this section are supplementary to limitations described or implicit in information given in other sections or on the drawings.

150   USE OF THE SITE:
–   Do not use the site for any purpose other than carrying out the Works.
–   Do not display or permit advertisements to be displayed on site without consent of the CA.

160   WORKING AREA for the Contractor will be confined to the new extension.

190   WORKING HOURS: 08.00 – 17.30

To collection £

A   Preliminaries/General conditions (continued)   £

A36   FACILITIES/TEMPORARY WORK/SERVICES

120   MAINTAIN, alter, adapt and move temporary works and services as necessary. Clear
         away when no longer required and make good.

421   LIGHTING AND POWER:
   –   The permanent electrical installation may be used by the Contractor.
   –   Electricity for the works will be supplied free of cost to the Contractor.

431   WATER for the Works will be supplied free of cost to the Contractor. Nature of supply:
         kitchen taps

440   TELEPHONE INSTALLATION: The Employer's existing telephone installation may be
         used by the Contractor.

A54   PROVISIONAL WORK/ITEMS

310   BUNK AND STORAGE FITTINGS:
   –   Include the Provisional Sum of £250.00

410   ELECTRICAL INSTALLATION to be executed by a specialist subcontractor selected by
         the CA:
   –   Include the net Provisional Sum of £1000.00
   –   Add for profit: _____%
   –   Allow for general attendance:
   –   Allow for the following special attendance: Power for small tools.

420   RESURFACING DRIVE to be executed by a specialist subcontractor selected by the
         CA:
   –   Include the net Provisional Sum of £1500.00
   –   Add for profit: _____%
   –   Allow for general attendance:

530   BUILDING CONTROL PRESCRIBED INSPECTION FEE:
         Include the Provisional Sum of £100.00

590   CONTINGENCIES:
         Include the Provisional Sum of £750.00

A55   DAYWORKS

110   LABOUR: Include Provisional Sums for:
   –   Prime cost of labour incurred before the Final Completion Date: The sum of £250.00
         Add for percentage adjustment: _____%
   –   Prime cost of labour incurred after the Final Completion Date: The sum of £250.00
         Add for percentage adjustment: _____%

120   MATERIALS AND GOODS: For prime cost incurred at any time during the Contract
         include the Provisional Sum of £250.00
         Add for percentage adjustment: _____%

130   PLANT: Include Provisional Sums for:
   –   Prime cost of plant incurred before the Final Completion Date: The sum of £100.00
         Add for percentage adjustment: _____%
   –   Prime cost of plant incurred after the Final Completion Date: The sum of £100.00
         Add for percentage adjustment: _____%
         (Rates for plant costs will be as set out in the Schedule of Basic Plant Charges
         published by the RICS current at the Date of Tender).

                                                         To collection £

£

B   SCHEDULE OF WORK

1   DEMOLITION/REMOVAL

1.1   Remove glass lean-to roof over existing carport together with timber plates, purlins, rafters, glazing bars, gutter, downpipe and flashing.

1.2   Take off and keep for reuse existing garage doors and ironmongery. Remove frame, fascia, and framing over.

1.3   Lift and keep for reuse paving slabs to path of no 112.

1.4   Remove half brick boundary wall between Nrs. 110 and 112 together with piers therein, rendered one brick wall and foundations under and prepare for erection of new party wall. Protect adjoining property and support retained earth.

1.5   Remove concrete ground floor to existing garage.

1.6   Move the metal storage bins clear of the boundary wall prior to demolition and adapt the timber top to the main coal bunkers including providing temporary back during rebuilding. Access to and full use of these bunkers will be required during winter months.

1.7   Remove staircase window and brickwork under and to one jamb to form enlarged door opening, face up jambs and make good all work disturbed.

2   FOUNDATIONS AND GROUND FLOOR

2.1   Excavate foundation trenches 600 mm deep D20

2.2   600 x 200 mm concrete foundation E10/10
       760 x 600 x 200 mm concrete pier foundation E10/10

2.3   250 mm cavity wall, common brickwork F10/30. Cavity fill F30/05.

2.4   Backfill up to garage floor and external paving formations with hardcore D20/65.

2.5   Relay precast slab paving to no. 112.

2.6   New concrete floor to carport, 100 mm thick laid to falls, mix E10/11, trowelled finish.

3   EXTERNAL WALLS

3.1   Facing brickwork F10/05 to outer leaf, inner leaf to carport and corner pier. Common brickwork F10/30 where not exposed to view. Brick on edge coping with tile creasing.

3.2   100 mm common blockwork F10/35 inner leaf.

3.3   50 mm cavity insulation F30/10

3.4   4 no air bricks F30/15

3.5   Stepped dpcs F30/30

3.6   250 x 230 RC beam, mix E10/11, two 12 mm diameter bars E30/10, fine smooth finish all faces.

To collection £

B   Schedule of Work (continued)   £

4   MAIN ROOF

4.1   150 x 50 joists G20/05 at 450 mm centres on joist hangers G20/65

4.2   50 mm wide firrings G20/10 at 450 mm centres to give fall of 1 in 10.

4.3   Plywood roof sheathing K11/10.

4.4   Warm deck roof covering J41/10

4.5   Lead flashing to existing house H71/35

4.6   76 mm gutter and 51 mm downpipe R10 discharging over lower level gutter.

5   FIRST FLOOR

5.1   150 x 150 joists G20/05 at 450 mm centres on joist hangers G20/65. Trimming round stair opening.

5.2   Timber board flooring K20/10.

5.3   50 mm thermal insulation P10/50.

6   EXTERNAL SCREENS AND FASCIAS

6.1   Purpose made screens to front and rear L10/15

6.2   19 mm plywood fascias to roof and floor (rear only) L10/15.

6.3   Bead double glazing L40/50.

6.4   Internal architraves and skirtings P20/10.

7   GLAZED ROOF AND GARAGE DOORS

7.1   100 x 50 mm rebated garage door frame L20/40.

7.2   Make good and reuse existing garage doors, including existing lock and handle, 2 pairs of new Collinges hinges to match existing.

7.3   50 x 32 mm twice rebated softwood glazing bars (timber as L10/15) framed in and prepared for glazing.

7.4   Putty glazing to roof L40/40.

7.5   Lead flashing to head and side abutments of glazed roof H71/35.

7.6   75 mm gutter and 76 mm downpipe R10 discharging over existing gully.

8   INTERNAL DOOR AND STAIR

8.1   Timber stair L30/10 fitted to prepared opening and existing landing with all necessary packings, trims and adaptations.

8.2   Door lining L20/41 with approved obscure glass fanlight and accordian door L20/60.

To collection £

B   Schedule of Work (continued)   £

9   FIXTURES

9.1   Wash basin N13/30.

9.2   38 mm copper waste carried through existing wall and connected to adjoining bedroom basin waste including cutting in and inserting 38 mm tee fitting.

9.3   Cut into existing 13 mm copper hot and cold water services under floor of adjoining bedroom, insert 13 mm tees and run 13 mm pipes through existing wall, within the depth of the new floor, then rising vertically. Joint to basin valves with 13 mm tap connectors and make good all work disturbed.

9.4   Provisional quantity of 3 sq m 19 mm oak shelving supplied and fixed as directed on and including a provisional amount of 6 m 50 x 50 mm oak framing.

10.0   ELECTRICAL INSTALLATION

10.1   A provisional sum is included at A54/410.

10.2   Cut away for and make good after electricians in all trades to the installation shown on the drawing, including switchgear, local switches, fittings and lamps. The conduit to lighting points will be embedded in the plaster, except in the carport where the conduit will be exposed.

11   FINISHES

11.1   Carport ceiling: fire resistant lining K11/60 on 50 x 50 mm battens, also to soffit and spandrels of stair.

11.2   First floor ceiling: plasterboard and skim M20/50

11.3   First floor walls: plaster M20/30 with V joint at junction of old and new walls.

11.4   First floor skirtings and architraves P20/10.

12   DECORATION

12.1   Carport walls not to be decorated.

12.2   Existing staircase not to be redecorated.

12.3   Emulsion M60/10 to the following:
           – Carport ceiling (nails not filled)
           – First floor walls and ceiling

12.4   Gloss M60/11 to the following:
           – Glazed roof bars and framing
           – Garage doors and frame.
           – First floor door frame and stair.
           – External screens and fascias.
           – Skirtings and architraves.

12.5   Wax polish oak shelving (provisional 6 sq m)

To collection £

£

PRICE COLLECTION

A   PRELIMINARIES/GENERAL CONDITIONS   Page   1

2

3

4

5

6

7

8

9

B   SCHEDULE OF WORK   Page   10

11

12

Carried to Form of Tender   £

13

D20   EXCAVATING AND FILLING

06   GROUND WATER LEVEL on the site is not known. Make all necessary enquiries concerning ground water level and allow for variations from that level.

15   BASIC WORKMANSHIP FOR EXCAVATING: Comply with BS 8000:Part 1, sections 3.1, 3.2 and 3.3.

25   FORMATIONS GENERALLY: Make advance arrangements with CA for inspection of formations for trench bottoms.

35   EXCESS EXCAVATIONS: Backfill any excavations taken:
–   Wider than required with material specified for backfilling.
–   Deeper than required with well graded granular material or lean mix concrete.

55   PLACING FILL GENERALLY:
–   Ensure that excavations and areas to be filled are free from loose soil, rubbish and water.
–   Do not use frozen materials or materials containing ice. Do not place fill on frozen surfaces.
–   Place and compact fill against structures, membranes or buried services in a sequence and manner which will ensure stability and avoid damage.
–   Plant employed for transporting, laying and compacting must be suited to the type of material.

65   HARDCORE:
–   Granular material, free from harmful matter, well graded, passing a 75 mm BS sieve and one of the following:
   –   Crushed hard rock or quarry waste (other than chalk).
   –   Crushed concrete, brick or tile, free from old plaster.
   –   Gravel or hoggin.
–   Spread and level backfilling in layers not exceeding 150 mm. Thoroughly compact each layer with power rammer or other suitable means.

E10   IN SITU CONCRETE

10   CONCRETE FOR FOUNDATIONS:
–   Ordinary prescribed mix to BS 5328, Grade C20P
–   Cement: Ordinary Portland cement.
–   Coarse and fine aggregates: To BS 882.
–   Nominal maximum size of aggregate: 20 mm.

11   CONCRETE FOR BEAMS AND
–   Ordinary prescribed mix to BS 5328, Grade C30P
–   Cement: Ordinary Portland cement.
–   Coarse and fine aggregates: To BS 882.
–   Nominal maximum size of aggregate: 20 mm.

30   MAKING CONCRETE GENERALLY:
–   Constituent materials, composition of mixes and production of concrete, sampling, testing and compliance to be in accordance with BS 5328 unless otherwise specified.
–   Use admixtures only if specified or approved.
–   Water content of concrete must be carefully controlled and adjusted to allow for moisture content of aggregates to give consistent quality and workability.
–   Ensure workability of concrete is such that it can be readily worked into corners and angles of forms and around reinforcement, constituent materials do not segregate and free water does not collect at the surface during placing.
–   Ready-mixed concrete may be used provided that it is obtained from a plant which holds a current Certificate of Accreditation under the Quality Scheme for Ready-mixed concrete. Cement contents higher than those specified in BS 5328 will be accepted.

E10   In situ concrete (continued)

40   MIXING ON SITE will be permitted as follows:
–   Mix proportions by volume: maximum amount of damp aggregate per 50 kg bag of cement:
     C20P: Fine 0.07 cu m, Coarse 0.13 cu m
–   Mix proportions by weight: maximum amounts of aggregate per 50 kg bag of cement:
     C20P: Fine 110 kg, Coarse 190 kg
     C30P: Fine 75 kg, Coarse 155 kg
–   Acceptable range of slump: 25–75 mm.

60   PLACING AND COMPACTING:
–   At time of placing ensure that all surfaces on which concrete is to be placed are clean, with no
     debris, tying wire clippings, fastenings or free water.
–   Place while sufficiently plastic for full compaction. Do not add water or retemper mixes. The
     temperature of concrete at time of placing must be not less than 5 degC. Do not place against
     frozen or frost covered surfaces.
–   Fully compact to full depth (until air bubbles cease to appear on the top surface), especially
     around reinforcement, cast-in accessories, into corners of formwork and at joints.

70   CURING AND PROTECTING:
–   Prevent surface evaporation from concrete surfaces as specified below by covering with
     polythene sheeting as soon as practicable after completion of placing and compacting,
     removing only to permit any finishing operations and replacing immediately thereafter:
     –   Surfaces which will be exposed to frost, and
          wearing surfaces of floors and pavements,
          regardless of weather conditions: not less than 10 days
     –   Other structural concrete surfaces: not less than 5 days.
–   Adequately protect concrete from shock, indentation and physical damage.

E20   FORMATIONS/FORMWORK FOR IN SITU CONCRETE

10   WORK BELOW GROUND: Vertical faces of strip footings, bases and slabs may be cast against
     faces of excavation, provided the faces are sufficiently accurate and stable and adequate
     measures are taken to prevent contamination of concrete.

40   FORMWORK:
–   Construct accurately and robustly to produce finished concrete to the required dimensions.
     Formed surfaces must be free from twist and bow, all intersections, lines and angles being
     square, plumb and true.
–   Construct (including joints between forms and completed work), to prevent loss of grout, using
     seals when necessary. Secure tight against adjacent concrete to prevent formation of steps.
–   Fix inserts or box out as required in correct positions before placing concrete. Form all holes
     and chases. Do not cut hardened concrete without approval.

E30   REINFORCEMENT FOR IN SITU CONCRETE

10   PLAIN BAR REINFORCEMENT FOR BEAMS: To BS 4449, Grade 250.

40   CLEANLINESS: At time of placing concrete, reinforcement to be clean and free of corrosive
     pitting, loose millscale, loose rust, ice and substances which may adversely affect the
     reinforcement, concrete, or bond between the two.

70   FIXING REINFORCEMENT:
–   Fix before the concrete is placed, providing suitable spacers at not more than 1 m centres or
     closer spacing as necessary to support in position and maintain the specified cover. Spacers to
     be not closer than 300 mm centres and staggered on adjacent parallel bars.
–   Fix adequately, using tying wire, which must not encroach into the concrete cover.

F10 BRICK/BLOCK WALLING

05   FACING BRICKWORK:
- Bricks: Calcium silicate to BS 187 Class 7
- Mortar: As section Z21, mix: 1:1:6
- Joints: Neat struck as the work proceeds.

30   COMMON BRICKWORK:
- Bricks: Calcium silicate to BS 187 Class 7.
- Mortar: As section Z21, mix: 1:1:6 above dpc level
                      1:3 below dpc level

35   COMMON BLOCKWORK:
- Blocks: Concrete to BS 6073:Part 1.
   Minimum average compressive strength: 7.0 N/sq mm
   Thermal resistance: Not less than 0.08 sq m degC/W at 3% moisture content.
   Work size: 440 x 215 x 100 mm
- Mortar: As section Z21, mix: 1:1:6

50   BASIC WORKMANSHIP:
- Comply with the clauses of BS 8000:Part 3 which are relevant to this section.
- Accuracy: Notwithstanding BS 8000:Part 3, clause 3.1.2, comply with Preliminaries A33/340 and any required critical dimensions given in the specification or on the drawings.

55   FACEWORK:
- Facework to start not less than 150 mm below finished level of external paving or soil.
- Select bricks/blocks with unchipped arrisses. Cut with a masonry saw where cut edges will be exposed to view.
- Build walls in stretching half lap bond when not specified otherwise.
- Keep courses evenly spaced using gauge rods. Set out carefully to ensure satisfactory junctions and joints with adjoining or built-in elements and components.
- Protect against damage and disfigurement, particularly arrisses of openings and corners.

60   ALTERATIONS/EXTENSIONS:
- Arrange brick courses to line up with existing work.
- Unless otherwise specified or agreed block bond new walls to existing by cutting pockets not less than 100 mm deep, the full thickness of the new wall, and:
   Brick to brick: 4 courses high at 8 course centres.
   Brick to block, block to brick or block to block: Every alternate block course.
   Bond new walling into pockets with all voids filled solid.
- Except where a straight vertical joint is specified, new and existing facework in the same plane to be tooth bonded together at every course to give a continuous appearance.
- Where new lintels or walling are to support existing structure, completely fill top joint with semidry mortar, hard packed and well rammed to ensure full load transfer after removal of temporary supports.

F30   ACCESSORIES/SUNDRY ITEMS FOR BRICK/BLOCK WALLING

05   CAVITIES:
- Fill cavities with concrete up to 225 mm below ground level dpc.
- Clean off surplus mortar from joints on cavity faces as the work proceeds. Keep cavities, ties and dpcs free from mortar and debris with laths or other suitable means.
- Leave perpends at 900 mm centres completely open in the brick course immediately above base of cavity, external openings and stepped dpcs. Provide not less than two weep holes over openings.

10   CAVITY INSULATION:
- Size to suit wall tie spacings, thickness: 50 mm.
  Manufacturer and reference: Stonewool Cavity Batts or equivalent.
- Fix securely to inner leaf as BS 8000:Part 3, clause 3.4.5.

15   AIR BRICKS: To BS 493, Class 1, 200 x 200 mm, colour to match facing bricks, built in as the work proceeds.

20   WALL TIES FOR CAVITIES IN MASONRY WALLS:
- To BS 1243, type: vertical twist
  Material/finish: galvanised mild steel
  Size to suit cavity width.
- Install as BS 8000:Part 3, clause 3.4.3.

30   BITUMEN DAMP PROOF COURSES AND CAVITY TRAYS: To BS 6398, class D

45   INSTALLATION OF DPCS/CAVITY TRAYS: Comply with the relevant clauses of BS 8000: Part 3, section 3.3.

G20   CARPENTRY/TIMBER FRAMING/FIRST FIXING

05   GRADED SOFTWOOD FOR FLOOR AND ROOF JOISTS:
- Stress graded to BS 4978 or other national equivalent and so marked.
  Strength class to BS 5268:Part 2: SC3
  Surface finish: Sawn
- Preservative treatment: As section Z12 and British Wood Preserving Association Commodity Specification C8

10   UNGRADED SOFTWOOD FOR FIRRINGS, ETC:
- Free from decay, insect attack (except pinholes borers) and with no knots wider than half the width of the section.
  Surface finish: Sawn
- Preservative treatment: As section Z12 and British Wood Preserving Association Commodity Specification C8

30   SELECTION AND USE OF TIMBER:
- Do not use timber members which are damaged, crushed or split beyond the limits permitted by their grading.
- Ensure that notches and holes are not so positioned in relation to knots or other defects that the strength of members will be reduced.
- Do not use scarf joints, finger joints or splice plates.

G20   Carpentry/Timber framing/First fixing (continued)

35   PROCESSING TREATED TIMBER:
–   Carry out as much cutting and machining as possible before treatment.
–   Retreat all treated timber which is sawn along the length, thicknessed, planed or otherwise extensively processed.
–   Treat timber surfaces exposed by minor cutting and drilling with two flood coats of a solution recommended for the purpose by main treatment solution manufacturer.

40   MOISTURE CONTENT of timber at time of erection to be not more than 24%

50   ADDITIONAL SUPPORTS:
–   Where not shown on drawings, position and fix additional studs, noggings or battens for appliances, fixtures, edges of sheets, etc., in accordance with manufacturers' recommendations.
–   All additional studs, noggings or battens to be of adequate size and have the same treatment, if any, as adjacent timber supports.

55   INSTALLING JOISTS GENERALLY:
–   Position at equal centres not exceeding designed spacing and true to level.
–   Install bowed joists with positive camber.

60   INSTALLING JOISTS ON HANGERS:
–   Bed hangers directly on and hard against supporting construction. Do not use packs or bed on mortar.
–   Cut joists to leave not more than 6 mm gap between ends of joists and back of hanger.
–   Rebate joists to lie flush with underside of hangers.
–   Fix joists to hangers with a nail in every hole.

65   JOIST HANGERS FOR FLOOR AND ROOF JOISTS:
      Material/finish: galvanised mild steel
      Size: To suit joist, design load and crushing strength of supporting construction.

70   TRIMMING OPENINGS: When not specified otherwise, trimmers and trimming joists to be not less than 25 mm wider than general joists.

H71   **LEAD SHEET FLASHINGS**

35   COVER FLASHINGS:
–   Lead: Code 4 in lengths not exceeding 1500 mm.
–   End to end joints: Laps of not less than 100 mm.
–   Cover: Not less than 100 mm.
–   Fixing to brickwork: Wedge into groove and point in mortar.
–   Fixing to timber: Close copper nail
–   Bottom edges: Clip at laps and 500 mm centres.

60   MATERIALS AND WORKMANSHIP GENERALLY:
–   Lead sheet: To BS 1178, colour marked for thickness and weight.
–   Cut, joint and dress lead neatly and accurately, to provide fully waterproof coverings/flashings, free from ripples, kinks, buckling and cracks.
–   Comply with good practice as described in the latest edition of 'Lead sheet in building' published by the Lead Development Association, unless agreed otherwise.
–   Do not use scribers or other sharp instruments to mark out lead and do not use solder.
–   Ensure that finished leadwork is fully supported, adequately fixed to resist wind uplift but also able to accommodate thermal movement without distortion or stress.
–   Finishing: Apply to all visible lead a smear coating of patination oil, evenly in one direction and in dry conditions.

J41   BUILT UP FELT ROOF COVERINGS

10   WARM DECK ROOF COVERING:
–   Base: Plywood
    Preparation: As clause 35
–   Insulation: CFC free PUR/PIR roofboard to BS 4841:Part 3 with composite cork overlay.
    Thickness: 50 mm.
    Laying: As clause 45.
–   Waterproof covering:
    Laying: As clause 50.
    First layer: BS 747 type 3G
    Attachment: Partial bonding as clause 60.
    Intermediate layer: BS 747 type 3B
    Top layer: BS 747 type 3B
–   Surface protection: Chippings as clause 95.

15   ROOFING GENERALLY:
–   Lay the full roof covering in a single operation to provide a secure, free draining and completely
    weathertight roof.
–   Ancillary products, primers and bonding agents, where not specified, to be types recommended
    for the purpose by the felt manufacturer.
–   Store felt indoors in reasonably warm conditions until immediately before use.
–   Provide temporary covers and drainage as required to keep unfinished areas of the roof dry.
–   Protect daywork joints in warm deck roofs with a lapped and fully bonded strip of top layer felt.

30   TIMBER FOR TRIMS, ETC:
–   Planed, free from wane, pitch pockets, decay and insect attack except pinhole borers.
–   Moisture content: Not more than 22% at time of covering.
–   Preservative treatment: CCA as British Wood Preserving Association Commodity Specification
    C8.
–   Fix with sherardized screws at not more than 600 mm centres.

35   PLYWOOD SLAB BASES: Cover joints between sheets with a 150 mm wide strip of felt, BS
     747 type 5U, centrally over joints and adhere to base with bonding compound along edges only.

45   WARM DECK INSULATION:
–   Lay boards with long edges at 45 degrees to structure, tightly butted with staggered end joints
    and in a full bed of bonding compound.
–   On completion of laying ensure that boards are in good condition, well fitting and with no
    springing or rocking.

50   LAYING FELT GENERALLY:
–   Unless specified otherwise lay sheets on hot bonding compound, ensuring a full bond with no
    air pockets.
–   Lay with not less than 50 mm side and 75 mm end laps, ensuring that water will drain over and
    not into laps. Leave a continuous bead of compound at laps of top layers.
–   Break bond with side laps staggered by one third sheet width in three layer coverings. Apply
    successive layers with minimum delay, ensuring that moisture is not trapped.
–   Form details with adequate overlapping, staggering of laps and full bonding so that they are
    waterproof.

60   PARTIAL BONDING: Loose lay the specified venting base layer to roof surfaces, but do not
     carry up angle fillets and vertical surfaces or through details.

J41   Built up felt roof coverings (continued)

70   UPSTANDS INCLUDING SKIRTINGS:
–   Angle fillets: Timber as clause 30.
–   Form upstands at ends of rolls by carrying felt up without using separate strip. Elsewhere use matching strips of felt, maintaining the specified laps.
–   Carry all layers to full height of upstand, fully bonding each layer. Where practicable carry top layer over top of upstand.
–   Where venting base layer felt is specified, stop at angle fillet and overlap onto upstand with strips of BS 747, type 3B felt fully bonded with 75 mm lap onto first layer.
–   Where the specified top layer of the roof will be covered by an applied finish, fully bond an additional layer of BS 747 Type 3B felt to upstand, lapped 75 mm onto horizontal surface of roof.

75   WELTED DRIPS:
–   Form using maximum length strips of mineral surfaced felt.
–   Bond or nail tail of welt to face of drip batten, fold neatly and bond welt together. Carry not less than 100 mm onto roof and overlap with top layer.

95   CHIPPINGS:
–   Pea gravel or crushed rock not less than 10 mm nominal size graded as 'Single sized aggregate for felt roofing', light coloured to approval.
–   Evenly pour dressing compound of 50 secs grade cut-back bitumen to BS 3690:Part 1 at 1.5 kg/sq m and scatter chippings at approximately 16 kg/sq m.
–   On completion remove loose chippings.

K11   RIGID SHEET SHEATHING/LININGS

10   PLYWOOD ROOF SHEATHING:
–   Base: Firrings at 450 mm centres
     Additional supports as clause 80.
–   Plywood: To BS 6566 or equivalent approved national standard.
     Thickness: 18 mm
     Bond type: WBP.
     Durability class: H.
     Face grain direction parallel to long edges.
     Edges: Square
–   Long edges running across supports
–   Fix at 150 mm centres along edges of boards and 300 mm centres along intermediate supports with 50 mm x 3 mm annular ring shank nails with anticorrosive finish.

60   BOARD CEILING LINING:
–   Base: 50 x 50 battens, additional supports at cross joints.
–   Manufacturer and reference: Fireboard MRX.
     Thickness: 6 mm
     Finish: textured
–   Long edges running with supports, end joints aligned.
–   Fix at 200 mm centres along edges of board and 200 mm centres along intermediate supports with 50 mm small headed rustproofed nails.
–   Joint treatment: close butted

80   ADDITIONAL SUPPORTS: Where specified ensure that studs/noggings/battens as specified in clause G20/50 and not less than 50 mm wide are provided as follows:
–   Tongue and groove jointed sheets: To all unsupported perimeter edges.
–   Butt jointed sheets: To all unsupported sheet edges.

K20   TIMBER BOARD FLOORING

10   TIMBER BOARD FLOORING:
- Boards: Tongued and grooved softwood to BS 1297.
  Finished size: 22 x 150 mm
  Moisture content at time of fixing: Not exceeding 19%.
- Fixing: As clause 50, secret nailed with 40 mm lost head nails.

50   FIXING BOARDS:
- Keep boards dry and do not fix to timber supports which have a moisture content greater than 18%.
- Do not fix boards internally until the building is weathertight.
- Nail each board securely to each support to give flat, true surfaces free from undulations, lipping, splits and protruding fastenings.
- Allow for movement of timber when positioning boards and fastenings to prevent cupping, springing, excessive opening of joints or other defects.
- Heading joints to be tightly butted and positioned centrally over supports, not less than two board widths apart on any one support.
- Neatly punch all exposed nail heads below surface and plane off any proud edges.

L10   EXTERNAL SCREENS

15   TIMBER SCREENS AND FASCIAS:
- Timber to BS 1186:Part 1.
  Species: Softwood
  Classes: Frames 3, sashes 2, beads 1 or CSH.
- Preservative treatment: Organic solvent with water repellant as BWPA Commodity Specification C5.
  Desired service life: 60 years.
- Joinery workmanship: As section Z10.
  Adhesive: Synthetic resin to BS 1204, type WBP.
  Moisture content on delivery: 16% +/-3
- Under sill panels:
  Plywood to BS 6566 or equivalent approved standard.
  Thickness: 19 mm
  Bond type: WBP.
  Durability class: H
  Surface grade: I or II
  Seal backs and edges before fixing
  50 mm insulation quilt
  12 mm plasterboard inner lining.
- Roof and floor fascias: 19 mm plywood as above.
- Glazing details: Beads as I 40/50
- Ironmongery/accessories: Brass hinges, SAA night notch fasteners and SAA casement stays.
- Finish as delivered: Prepare and prime as M60/11
- Fixing: Cramps as section Z20.

75   SEALANT JOINTS:
- Sealant manufacturer and reference: Sealmaster Butyl
  Colour: White
- Prepare joints and apply sealant as section Z22.

80   IRONMONGERY: Fix carefully using fastenings with matching finish supplied by ironmongery manufacturer. Prevent damage to ironmongery and adjacent surfaces.

L20   DOORS

40   GARAGE DOOR FRAME:
–   Timber to BS 1186:Part 1.
        Species: Softwood
        Class: 3
–   Preservative treatment: Organic solvent with water repellant as BWPA Commodity Specification
        C5.
        Desired service life: 60 years
–   Joinery workmanship: As section Z10.
        Adhesive: Synthetic resin to BS 1204, type WBP
        Moisture content on delivery: 16% +/- 3
        Finish as delivered: Prepare and prime as M60/11
–   Fixing: Cramps as section Z20.

41   INTERNAL DOOR LINING:
–   Timber to BS 1186:Part 1.
        Species: Softwood
        Class: 3.
–   Detailing: 40 mm thick, cross tongued, full depth of opening, plain architraves P20/10. Door
        head to fanlight to be as manufacturer's recommended detail to suit door L20/60.
–   Joinery workmanship: As section Z10.
        Adhesive: Synthetic resin to BS 1204, type WBP
        Moisture content on delivery: 15% +/- 2
–   Finish as delivered: Prepare and prime as M60/11
–   Fixing: Plugged and screwed as section Z20.

60   ACCORDION DOOR FROM STAIR:
        Manufacturer and reference: Pillar 'Princess'
        Finish: Stained ash lacquered veneer
        Size: to be measured on site.

80   SEALANT JOINTS TO GARAGE DOORS:
–   Sealant manufacturer and reference: Sealmaster Butyl
        Colour: White
–   Prepare joints and apply sealant as section Z22.

L30   STAIRS

10   TIMBER STAIRS:
–   To BS 585.
        Moisture content on delivery: 10% +/-2%
–   Balustrade: Softwood newel, rail and balusters one side only.
–   Finish as delivered: Prepare and prime as M60/11.

60   FIXING GENERALLY:
–   Methods of fixing and fastenings to be as section Z20 unless specified otherwise.
–   Do not modify, cut, notch or make holes in structural members except as shown on drawings or
        as approved.

L40   GLAZING

10   WORKMANSHIP GENERALLY:
- Glass generally to BS 952, free from cracks, rippling, dimples and other defects.
- All surfaces to receive glazing to be clean, dry and free from grease at time of priming/sealing and glazing. Prime/seal if recommended by glazing compound manufacturer.
- Ensure that glazing materials, surrounds, primers, etc, used together are compatible.
- Comply with BS 6262 and glass and sealant manufacturers' recommendations for edge cover and clearance, positions and materials of distance pieces, setting and location blocks.

40   PUTTY FRONTED GLAZING TO GLASS ROOF:
- Pane material: 6 mm clear float glass
- Surround: Timber
- Putty: To BS 544.
- Fully bed panes in putty not less than 1.5 mm thick and secure with glazier's sprigs at 300 mm centres. Form front putty to a neat triangular fillet stopping 2 mm short of sightline and leave smooth with no brush marks.
- Apply at least one coat of the final finish as soon as putty is sufficiently hard and not more than 28 days after glazing.

50   BEAD DOUBLE GLAZING TO EXTERNAL SCREENS:
- Pane material: Units to BS 5713, 6 mm clear float both sides.
- Surround/bead: Softwood frame with hardwood beads.
- Glazing compound: Glazza wood grade.
- Fully bed panes and beads in compound not less than 3 mm thick and fix beads with brass panel pins at 150 mm centres starting not more than 50 mm from each corner. Trim excess compound to form a smooth, neat chamfer.

M20   PLASTERED COATINGS

30   LIGHTWEIGHT GYPSUM PLASTER:
- Background: new blockwork and existing brickwork.
- Undercoats(s):
  Premixed lightweight browning plaster to BS 1191:Part 2.
  Thickness (excluding dubbing out): 11 mm
- Final coat:
  Premixed lightweight finish plaster to BS 1191:Part 2.
  Thickness: 2 mm
  Finish: Smooth.

50   PLASTERBOARD AND SKIM:
- Background: Joists at 450 mm centres
- Plasterboard backing: 9.5 mm gypsum baseboard with aluminium foil backing, nail fixed.
- Skim coat:
  Board finish plaster: To BS 1191:Part 1, Class B.
  Thickness: 5 mm applied in 2 coats.
  Finish: Smooth.

60   BASIC WORKMANSHIP:
- Comply with the clauses of BS 8000:Part 10 which are relevant to this section.
- Provide appropriate beads/stops at all external angles and stop ends unless specified otherwise.

80   PLASTERBOARD BACKINGS:
- Ensure that bearers, etc. to support fittings and services are accurately and securely fixed.
- In addition to the requirements of BS 8000:Part 10, ensure that all edges of vapour check and fire resisting backing are fully supported.

86   JOINTS BETWEEN BOARDS AND SOLID BACKGROUNDS which are both to be plastered:
Fill and scrim unless specified otherwise.

M60 PAINTING

10 EMULSION:
- Manufacturer: Brolux
- Surface(s): Plaster and fire resistant board.
  Preparation: As clause 30.
- Initial coat(s): 1 thinned emulsion
- Finishing coats: 2 Vinsilk Emulsion

11 GLOSS:
- Manufacturer: Brolux
- Surface(s): timber
  Preparation: As clause 30.
- Initial coat(s): Aluminium wood primer, 1 undercoat
- Finishing coats: 2 Weatherflex Gloss

30 PREPARATION GENERALLY:
- Comply with BS 8000:Part 12, Section 2 and additional requirements in this specification.
- When removing or partially removing coatings, use methods which will not damage the substrate or adjacent surfaces or adversely affect subsequent coatings.
- Materials used in preparation to be types recommended by their manufacturers and the coating manufacturer for the situation and surfaces being prepared.
- Apply oil based stoppers/fillers after priming. Apply water based stoppers/fillers before priming unless recommended otherwise by manufacturer. Patch prime water based stoppers/fillers when applied after priming.
- Ensure that doors and opening windows, etc., are 'eased' as necessary before coating. Prime any resulting bare areas.

60 PAINTING GENERALLY: Comply with BS 8000:Part 12, Section 3.2 and additional requirements of this specification.

77 BEAD GLAZING: Joinery which is to be painted must have the primer and one undercoat applied to rebates and beads before glazing.

80 PUTTY GLAZING: Allow putty to set for 7 days then, within a further 14 days, seal with an oil based primer. Ensure that putty is fully protected by coating system as soon as it is sufficiently hard. Extend finishing coats on to glass up to sight line.

90 COMPLETION: Ensure that opening lights and other moving parts move freely. Remove all masking tape and temporary coverings.

N13 SANITARY APPLIANCES/FITTINGS

30 WASH BASIN:
- Type: Vitreous china 560 x 405 mm to BS 1188
- Taps: 12 mm Chromium plated raised nose pillar taps.
- Waste: 32 mm Bead chain waste and plug 80 mm slotted tail.
- Trap: 32 mm white plastic
- Other accessories: wall brackets.

70 INSTALLATION GENERALLY:
- To BS 8000:Part 13, clause 3.2.
- Form watertight joints using jointing and bedding compounds recommended by the manufacturers of the appliances, accessories and pipes being jointed or bedded.
- Prevent use of appliance for any purpose until Practical Completion.

P10   SUNDRY INSULATION

50   FIBRE INSULATION SUPPORTED BETWEEN FLOOR JOISTS:
–   Manufacturer and reference: Woolymat Extra or equivalent.
Thickness: 50 mm
–   Drape and staple 20–25 mm square mesh polyethylene net over joists. Lay insulation on net between joists, leaving a 25 mm space between top and underside of flooring.

P20   UNFRAMED ISOLATED TRIMS/SKIRTINGS/SUNDRY ITEMS

10   SOFTWOOD SKIRTINGS, DOOR AND EXTERNAL SCREEN ARCHITRAVES:
–   To BS 584.
Class (BS 1186:Part 1): 2
Moisture content on delivery: 15% +/- 2
–   Architraves: 100 x 25 mm
–   Skirtings: 125 x 25 mm
–   Fixing: Nailed at 450 mm centres

50   INSTALLATION GENERALLY:
–   Methods of fixing and fastenings to be as section Z20 unless specified otherwise.
–   Straight runs to be formed in single lengths wherever possible. Location and method of forming running joints to be approved by the CA where not detailed.
–   All joints at angles to be mitred unless specified otherwise.
–   Moisture content of timber and wood based boards to be maintained during storage and installation within the range specified for the component.

R10   RAINWATER PIPEWORK/GUTTERS

20   PLASTICS PIPEWORK:
–   Pipes, fittings and accessories: UPVC.
Manufacturer and reference: to be approved
Shape: Round, 51 and 76 mm diameter
Colour: Black
Accessories: Shoe, 100 degree bend
–   Fixing: Proprietary clips at 2500 mm centres.

25   PLASTICS GUTTERS:
–   Gutters and fittings: UPVC.
Manufacturer and reference: to be approved
Profile: Half round 76 mm
Colour: Black
–   Fixing: Proprietary brackets at 900 mm centres.

50   INSTALLATION GENERALLY:
–   Install in accordance with BS 8000:Part 13, Section 3 to ensure the complete discharge of rainwater from the building without leaking.
–   Obtain all components for each type of pipework/guttering from the same manufacturer.
–   Where not specified otherwise use plated, sherardized, galvanized or nonferrous fastenings, suitable for the purpose and background, and compatible with the material being fixed.

60   GUTTERS:
–   Set out to a true line to ensure no ponding or backfall. Position high points of gutters as close as practical to the roof and low points not more than 50 mm below the roof.
–   Overlap joints in direction of fall and seal as specified to make watertight.
–   Ensure that roofing underlay is dressed into gutter.

70   PIPEWORK:
–   Fix securely at specified centres providing additional supports as necessary to support pipe collars, particularly at changes in direction.
–   Make changes in direction of pipe runs only where shown on drawings.

Z10   PURPOSE MADE JOINERY

10   FABRICATION GENERALLY:
– Fabricate joinery components to BS 1186:Part 2.
– Form sections out of the solid when not specified otherwise. Carefully machine timber to accurate lengths and profiles, free from twist and bowing. After machining, surfaces to be smooth and free from tearing, woolliness, chip bruising and other machining defects.
– Assemble with tight, close fitting joints to produce rigid components free from distortion.
– Screw heads to be countersunk not less than 2 mm below timber surfaces which will be visible in completed work. All screws to have clearance holes.

20   CROSS SECTION DIMENSIONS of timber are nominal sizes unless stated otherwise. Reduction to finished sizes to be to BS 4471 for softwoods and BS 5450 for hardwoods. Deviation from the stated sizes will not be permitted unless prior approval is given.

30   PRESERVATIVE TREATED TIMBER:
– Carry out as much cutting and machining as possible before treatment.
– Retreat all timber which is sawn along the length, ploughed, thicknessed, planed or otherwise extensively processed.
– Treat surfaces exposed by minor cutting and drilling with two flood coats of a solution recommended for the purpose by main treatment solution manufacturer.

40   MOISTURE CONTENT of timber and wood based sheets to be maintained during manufacture and storage, within the range specified for the component.

50   FINISHING AND PROTECTING:
– Sand all joinery to give smooth, flat surfaces suitable to receive specified finishes. Arrisses to be eased unless specified otherwise.
– Before assembly, seal exposed end grain of external components with aluminium primer or clear sealer as appropriate and allow to dry.
– Protect completed joinery against damage, dirt, moisture and other deleterious substances.

Z20   FIXINGS

10   FIXING GENERALLY: Use fixing and jointing methods and types, sizes, quantities and spacings of fastenings which are suitable having regard to:
– Nature of and compatibility with product/material being fixed and fixed to,
– Recommendations of manufacturers of fastenings and manufacturers of components, products or materials being fixed and fixed to,
– Materials and loads to be supported,
– Conditions expected in use,
– Appearance, this being subject to approval.

20   FASTENINGS for materials and components forming part of external construction to be of corrosion resistant material or have a corrosion resistant finish.

30   FIXING THROUGH FINISHES: Ensure that fastenings and plugs (if used) have ample penetration into the backing.

40   CRAMP FIXING:
– Fix with stainless or galvanized steel strip cramps as BS 1243 vertical twist ties except with no twist, split one end only and once bent.
– Position cramps 150 mm from each end of jambs and at 600 mm maximum centres.
– Secure cramps to frames with two sherardized screws and fully bed in mortar.

Z21   MORTARS

10   MORTAR MIX PROPORTIONS and other particular requirements are specified elsewhere.

20   SAND FOR MORTAR:
–   To BS 1200 unless specified otherwise.
–   Sand for facework mortar to be from one source, different loads to be mixed if necessary to ensure consistency of colour and texture.

30   LIME BASED MORTARS: Use ready-mixed lime:sand to BS 4721.

40   CEMENT FOR MORTAR: When not specified otherwise, to be ordinary or rapid hardening Portland cement or blastfurnace cement. All cements must comply with the appropriate British Standard and be manufactured by a BSI Registered Firm of Assessed Capability.

50   ADMIXTURES: Do not use in mortar unless specified or approved. Do not use calcium chloride or any admixtures containing calcium chloride. Admixtures, if specified, to be to BS 4887.

60   MAKING MORTAR:
–   Measure materials accurately by volume using clean gauge boxes. Proportions of mixes are for dry sand; allow for bulking if sand is damp.
–   Mix ingredients thoroughly to a consistence suitable for the work and free from lumps. Do not overmix mortars containing air entraining admixtures.
–   Use mortar within about two hours of mixing at normal temperatures. Do not use after the initial set has taken place and do not retemper.
–   Keep plant and banker boards clean at all times.

Z22   SEALANTS

10   SEALANT TYPES: As specified in the relevant section.

20   SUITABILITY OF JOINTS: Before commencing, check that:
    –   Joint dimensions are within limits specified for the sealant.
    –   Surfaces are smooth and undamaged.
    –   Preparatory work which must be done before assembly of the joint has been carried out.
Inform CA if joints are not suitable to receive sealant and submit proposals for rectification.

30   PREPARING JOINTS:
–   Remove all temporary coatings, tapes, loosely adhering material, dust, oil, grease and other contaminants which may affect bond.
–   Backing strip, bond breaker, primer: Types recommended for the purpose by sealant manufacturer.
–   Insert backing strips and/or bond breaker tape into joint leaving no gaps.
–   Cover adjacent surfaces with masking tape to prevent staining and protect surfaces which would be difficult to clean if smeared with primer or sealant.

40   APPLYING SEALANTS:
–   Do not apply to damp surfaces (unless recommended otherwise), to surfaces affected by ice or snow or during inclement weather. Do not heat joints to dry them or raise the temperature.
–   Fill joints completely, leaving no gaps, excluding all air and ensuring firm adhesion of sealant to required joint surfaces. Tool the sealant to a neat, slightly concave profile unless specified otherwise.

Index

Italics refer to Common Arrangement of Work Sections for building works – references restricted to first and second levels.

Air conditioning systems, *U*, 97
Alterations composite items, *C2*, 41, 116
   works of, 8
Asphalt coatings, *J2*, 62
Authorship of specification, 14

Balustrades, *L3*, 69
Bill of quantities link with specification, 21
Brick and block walling, *F1*, 49, 122
   example specifications (NBS), 25
British standards, 10, 33
Building fabric reference,
   specification, *Z*, 103
   sundries, *P*, 81, 131
Building owners materials, 12, 37
Building regulations, 9

Carcassing,
   metal, *G1*, 54
   timber, *G2*, 55, 123
Cladding/covering glazed, *H1*, 58
   malleable sheet, *H7*, 60, 124
   profiled sheet, *H3*, 58
   slate, *H6*, 59
   tile, *H6*, 59
Clause headings, 18
Clerk of Works specification for, 3
Codes of practice, 10, 33
Communication systems, *W*, 99
Common Arrangement, 15
Complete buildings, *B*, 39
Composition and style, 14
Concrete precast, *E5*, 47
   in situ, *E1*, 44, 120
Consistency in specification, 18
Control systems, *W*, 99
Cooling systems, *T*, 95
Co-ordinating committee, 15
Complete buildings, *B*, 39

Date, keeping up to, 13
Decking metal/timber, *G3*, 56
Demolition, *C1*, 40, 116
Disposal systems, *R*, 86, 131
Doors, *L2*, 68, 115
Drafting procedures, 17
Drainage, *R1*, 86
Drawings, matters for, 7
Dry partitions, *K3*, 65

Edging to pavings, *Q1*, 83
Electrical services, 115, 118
   supply, *V*, 98
Engineering services work in connection, *P3*, 82
Equipment, *N1*, 78
Example specification, 104
   table of contents, 106
Excavation, *D2*, 42, 120

Fabric building reference specification, *Z*, 103
False ceilings, *K4*, 65
Felt/flexible sheets, *J4*, 63, 125
Fencing, *Q4*, 85
Filling, *D2*, 42
Finishes sundry, *P2*, 81
   surface, *M*, 71, 118
Fittings, *P2*, 81
Fixtures, *N1*, 78, 118
Flexible sheet/tile coverings, *M5*, 75
Flooring trowelled, *M1*, 71
Form of specification, 14
Formwork, *F2*, 46, 121
Foundations, specification of, 6
Furnishings, *N1*, 78, 115
Furniture site, *Q5*, 85
   equipment, *N*, 78, 115

Galleries, *L3*, 69
Gas supply, *S3*, 93
General conditions, *A*, 35, 107
Glazed cladding/covering, *H1*, 58
Glazing, *L4*, 70, 117, 129
Ground works, *D*, 120

Hatches, *L2*, 68
Heating mechanical, *T*, 95

Index of specification, 20
In situ concrete, *E*, 44, 120
Insulation, *P1*, 81
Ironmongery, *P2*, 82

Lighting systems, *V*, 98
Linings, *K*, 64
   board, *K2*, 65
   dry, *K3*, 65
   rigid sheet, *K1*, 64
Louvres, *L1*, 66

Malleable sheet coverings/claddings, *H7*, 60
Masonry, *F*, 49, 122
  accessories, *F3*, 52
Materials clauses, building owner's own, 12
Metal decking, *G3*, 56
  structures, *G1*, 54

National Building Specifications, 23
Nominated subcontractors/suppliers, 9, 38
Numbering specifications, 18

Painting, *K6*, 76, 118, 130
Partitioning dry, *K3*, 65
Pavings, *Q2*, 84, 113
  edgings, *Q1*, 83
P.C. prices, 8
Piped supply systems, *S*, 91
Planting, *Q3*, 84
Plastered coatings, *M2*, 72, 129
  work related to, *M3*, 73
Power systems, *V*, 73, 98
Precast concrete large, *E5*, 48
Preliminaries, *A*, 35, 107
Preliminary Items, 13, 17
Production Drawings Code, 7
Profiled sheet cladding, *H3*, 58
Project Specification Code, 16
Proofs of specification, 22
Provisional sums generally, 8, 38, 115
  statutory charges, 10, 38
Purpose of specification, 1

Quantity surveyors
  specification for, 3

Refrigeration systems, *T*, 95
Refuse disposal, *R3*, 90
Reinforcement, *E3*, 46, 121
Renovations, *C*, 40
Reproduction of specifications, 21
Rooflights, *L1*, 66

Sanitary appliances, 118
Schedules, 19, 116
Screeds, *M1*, 71
Screens, *L1*, 66, 127
Security systems, *W*, 99
Services reference specification, *Y*, 101
Sewerage, *R2*, 90
Sheathings, *K*, 64
  board, *K2*, 65
  rigid sheet, *K1*, 64
Sheet flexible coverings, *M5*, 75, 126
Shutters, *L2*, 68
Site agent, specification for, 3
Site furniture, *Q5*, 85
  planting, *Q3*, 84
Slate cladding, *H6*, 59
Specification,
  authorship, 14
  basis for tenders, 2
  building owner's materials, 12, 37
  clause headings, 18
  Clerk of Works, for, 3
  composition and style, 14

consistency, 18
contents, 4
essentials in writing, 4
form of, 14
foundations, 6
index, 20
keeping up to date, 13
link with bill of quantities, 21
numbering, 18
P.C. prices, 8
Preliminary Items, 12, 17
proofs, 22
provisional sums, 8, 38
purpose of, 1
quantity surveyor for, 3
reproduction, 21
schedules, 19
site agent for, 3
standardisation of form, 20
sub-divisions of, 8
subject-matter for, 7
terminology, 16
underlining, 18
use of, 1, 10
what is it for?, 2
workmanship clauses, 11
works of alteration, 8
Stairs, *L3*, 69, 128
Standard specification use of, 10
Standardisation of form, 20
Statutory charges, provision for, 10, 38
Stone walling, *F2*, 51
Structural carcassing metal, *G1*, 54
  timber, *G2*, 123
Sub-division of specification, 8
Subject-matter for specification, 7
Supply systems electrical, *V*, 98
  gas, *S3*, 93
  piped, *S*, 91
  water, *S1*, 91
Surface finishes, *M*, 71, 129

Tenders specification as basis for, 2
Terminology, 16
Thesaurus Construction Industry, 17
Tile cladding, *H6*, 59
  coverings flexible, *M5*, 75
  rigid, *M4*, 74
Timber decking, *G3*, 56
  structural carcassing, *G2*, 55, 123
Transport systems, *X*, 100

Underlining in specifications, 18
Underpinning, *D5*, 43
Use of specification, 1, 10

Ventilation systems, *U*, 97

Walkways, *L3*, 69
Waterproofing, *J*, 62, 125
Water supply, *S1*, 91
Windows, *L1*, 66, 127
Workmanship clauses, 11
Writing, essentials in, 4